你好

Nǐ Hǎo

①

Chinese Language Course

Introductory Level

by

Shumang Fredlein ● Paul Fredlein

ChinaSoft

Nǐ Hǎo 1 – Chinese Language Course – Introductory level
Published 1991; reprinted 1993, 1994, 1995, 1996, 1997, 1999
New edition 2001; reprinted 2002, 2003, 2004, 2005, 2006, 2007

ChinaSoft Pty Ltd   ABN: 61 083 458 459
P.O. Box 845, Toowong, Brisbane, Qld 4066, AUSTRALIA
Telephone   (61-7) 3371-7436
Facsimile   (61-7) 3371-6711
www.chinasoft.com.au

Written by Shumang Fredlein (林淑满) & Paul Fredlein
Illustrated by Xiaolin Xue (薛曉林), Zhengdong Su (苏正东), Bo Wu (吴波), Xudong Zhu (朱旭东)
Edited by Sitong Jan (詹絲桐), Xiaolin Xue (薛曉林)
Typeset by ChinaSoft on Apple Macintosh

Printed in Australia by Watson Ferguson & Company, Brisbane

Companion workbook, audio CDs, audio tapes and Games software also available.

ISBN 978 1 876739 06 5

Preface

It has been ten years since the Ni Hao series was first published. I am glad that it has been receiving such strong support from teachers and students throughout the world. Many have shown their approval and provided us with advice and suggestions. It is our goal to keep improving the series. This new edition is our attempt to achieve this goal.

In Ni Hao 1, there are more reading materials linking and consolidating the language introduced in different lessons. These new items are spiced with humour to make learning more interesting. Another print colour is also added to make the book more appealing.

The revision work has been made easier with new members joining the editing team. Thanks to Sitong and Xiaolin who contribute their professional skills and knowledge in all areas needed. Their devotion and effort has smoothed the working process. Paul's interest in programming has turned the Ni Hao series into a multimedia integrated language learning course and has made the series more complete.

I would like to thank my daughter Jemma and my son David who grew up with the books. Watching their learning process and hearing their comments on the books always sparks me with new ideas.

Many thanks are owed to Juanita Yuan who provided us with teaching material at the beginning stage. I would also like to thank Lin Song, Peter Chan, Lily Dong, Chris Kain, Jessy Tu, Lisa Allen and many other teachers, who provided their advice and suggestions that led to the new look of this edition.

Shumang, 2001

Contents

Introduction

你好 Nǐ Hǎo is a basic course for beginning students of Chinese. It introduces Chinese language and culture and aims to teach communication in both spoken and written Chinese. The objectives are to enable students to use Chinese in the classroom, playground, local community and countries where the Chinese language is spoken.

The text is richly illustrated, providing a stimulating language learning tool to motivate students. Characters are used throughout the text to enhance the students' reading and writing ability. Pinyin only acts as a guide to pronunciation. When it appears on top of the characters, no capital letter is used at the beginning of the sentence and no full stop is employed. As learning progresses, the Pinyin of the characters that students have learnt is omitted. To equip students to read authentic materials, various print fonts are used: Kǎishū [楷书], used in the main text, is an ideal font for students to learn to write; Sòngtǐ [宋体], used in the sentence patterns, is a font commonly used in newspapers and general publications; while Hēitǐ [黑体] is only used for titles. Apart from print fonts, various hand-written scripts are included to provide students with the opportunity to read handwriting. To make students aware of the current use of traditional characters in Taiwan and overseas Chinese communities, the traditional form is included in the vocabulary list in the appendix.

Each unit of the text in this book includes the subsections:

> *Illustrated texts*
> *Learn the sentences*
> *New words and expressions*
> *Write the characters*
> *Supplementary words*
> *Something to know*

In *Illustrated texts*, each conversation is based on daily life with the language in a spiralled structure. The illustrations assist in the interpretation of the conversation and are ideally suited to role playing. Grammar explanations in *Learn the sentences* are simple and illustrated with examples to clarify usage. Students can also use this section to hold conversations with partners. In *New words and expressions*, the meaning of the separate characters in each word will assist students to understand the structure of the word. The section *Supplementary words* provides students who progress quickly with additional learning material. Characters that the students should learn to write have the stroke order clearly illustrated in *Write the characters*. It is essential to write characters in the correct stroke order. Culture related to the content of the lesson is introduced in *Something to know*, a section designed to enrich cultural understanding and generate interest in learning the language.

In addition to the six subsections, songs, rhymes, tongue twisters, cartoons, little stories and interesting features of Chinese characters also play important roles in the book. They are light and cheerful materials offering wonderful opportunities for practice and reinforcement.

The Ni Hao series is a complete learning course which comprises five levels. Each level contains a textbook, a workbook, a teacher's handbook, a set of audio cassettes (or CDs), a CD-ROM games software and a CD-ROM language lab software. The textbook – An Introduction to Chinese – features the basic daily language in various topics and settings and is structured, accumulative and reinforced. The student workbook contains a variety of tasks and activities using all four communication skills. The audio cassettes include all language sections in the book and the listening comprehension sections in the workbook. The handbook provides the teacher notes, suggested activities and materials that can be reproduced for class use including worksheets and flashcards. The games software allows students to revise the use of language in different settings, to use the mouse to write characters in the correct stroke order, and to challenge their memory in phrases and characters. The language lab software moves the traditional language lab to the personal computer. It allows students to interact while listening, repeating or role-playing. Students' voice can be recorded and replayed. Both programs are ideal for either class use or students' personal use.

For students who wish to learn traditional characters, the traditional character edition of the textbooks and workbooks are published by Cheng & Tsui Company in the USA under licence from ChinaSoft.

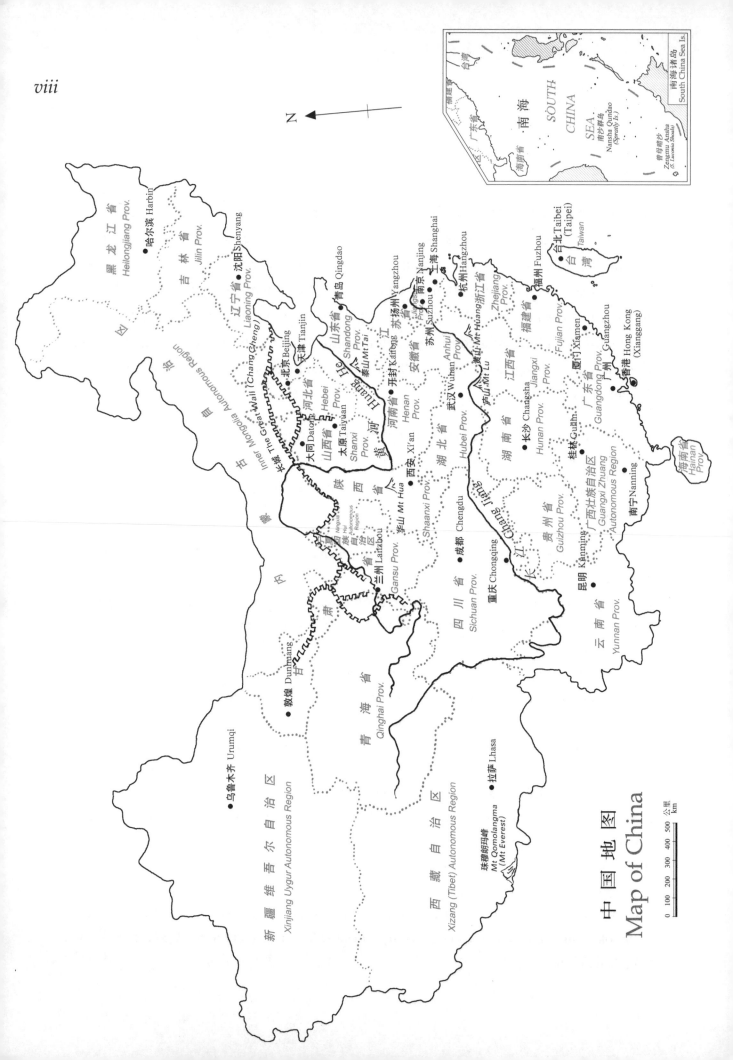

N

南海诸岛
South China Sea Is.

台湾
Taiwan

福建省
Fujian Prov.

广东省
Guangdong Prov.

海南省
Hainan Prov.

SOUTH
CHINA
SEA

南海

南沙群岛
Nantsha Quntao
(Spratly Is.)

曾母暗沙
Zengmu Ansha
(S. Luconia Shoals)

哈尔滨 Harbin

黑 龙 江 省
Heilongjiang Prov.

吉 林 省
Jilin Prov.

沈阳 Shenyang

辽 宁 省
Liaoning Prov.

内 蒙 古 自 治 区
Inner Mongolia Autonomous Region

长城 The Great Wall (Chang Cheng)

北京 Beijing

天津 Tianjin

河北省 Hebei Prov.

大同 Datong

山西省 Shanxi Prov.

太原 Taiyuan

山东省
Shandong Prov.

青岛 Qingdao

泰山 Mt Tai

开封 Kaifeng

河南省 Henan Prov.

西安 Xi'an

陕 西 省 Shaanxi Prov.

华山 Mt Hua

宁夏回族自治区 Ningxia Hui Autonomous Region

兰州 Lanzhou

甘肃省 Gansu Prov.

敦煌 Dunhuang

青 海 省
Qinghai Prov.

乌鲁木齐 Urumqi

新 疆 维 吾 尔 自 治 区
Xinjiang Uygur Autonomous Region

西 藏 自 治 区
Xizang (Tibet) Autonomous Region

珠穆朗玛峰
Mt Qomolangma
(Mt Everest)

拉萨 Lhasa

四 川 省
Sichuan Prov.

成都 Chengdu

重庆 Chongqing

云 南 省
Yunnan Prov.

昆明 Kunming

贵 州 省
Guizhou Prov.

广西壮族自治区
Guangxi Zhuang
Autonomous Region

南宁 Nanning

桂林 Guilin

湖 南 省
Hunan Prov.

长沙 Changsha

湖 北 省
Hubei Prov.

武汉 Wuhan

长 江 Chang Jiang

江 西 省
Jiangxi Prov.

庐山 Mt Lu

广 东 省
Guangdong Prov.

广州 Guangzhou

香港 Hong Kong
(Xianggang)

厦门 Xiamen

福建省
Fujian Prov.

福州 Fuzhou

浙江省 Zhejiang Prov.

杭州 Hangzhou

黄山 Mt Huang

安徽省 Anhui Prov.

江苏省 Jiangsu Prov.

苏州 Suzhou

南京 Nanjing

上海 Shanghai

扬州 Yangzhou

台北 Taibei
(Taipei)

中 国 地 图
Map of China

0 100 200 300 400 500
公里
km

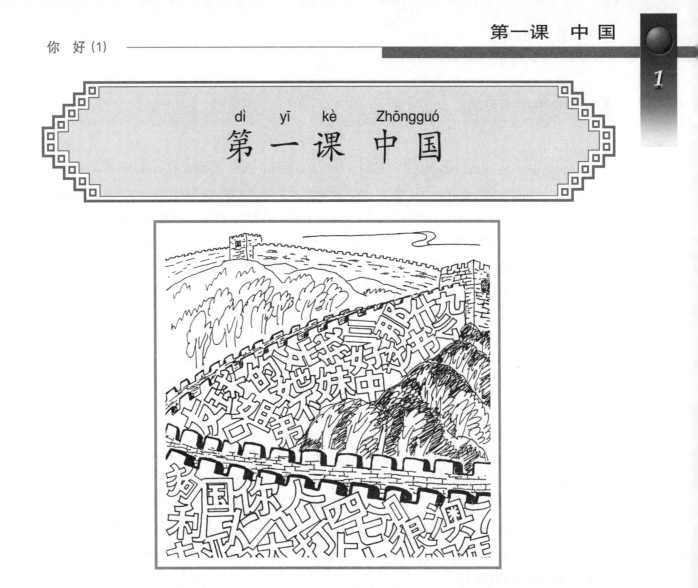

dì　yī　kè　Zhōngguó
第 一 课 中 国

1 The country

China is situated in the eastern part of the Asian continent and is the third largest country in the world. It covers a total area of approximately 9.6 million square kilometres and is a land of contrasts with deserts in the north, mountains in the south and cultivated areas in the east.

This vast land supports almost a quarter of the world's population: over one billion people of different races, traditions and cultures. Although the majority (about 94% of the population) are the Han people, there are fifty-five minority peoples, the largest among them being the Mongolians [Ménggǔzú 蒙古族], the Tibetans [Zàngzú 藏族] and the Zhuang [Zhuàngzú 壮族].

Chinese culture was the cradle of Japanese, Korean and some South East Asian cultures. The ancient Chinese considered their country to be the centre of the world and called it Zhōngguó [中国], literally meaning 'the Central Kingdom'.

2 The language

There are variations in the language of China because of its great distances and the diversity of its people. Some minority peoples use their own language which differs from the traditional Chinese language. Those who use the traditional language (around 80% of the Chinese population) have developed regional differences in pronunciation, words and grammar. These variations are called *dialects*. People who speak one dialect sometimes find it difficult to understand the speech of someone who speaks another. Just as an Australian might have difficulty understanding a strong Scottish accent, so too people who only speak Cantonese [Guǎngdōnghuà 广东话] may have trouble talking with people who only speak the Min dialect [Fújiànhuà 福建话]. However, people who speak different dialects can always communicate with each other in the written language, which was unified by the First Emperor [Qín Shǐhuáng 秦始皇] (221–210 BC).

Although the written Chinese language was the same, there were still problems in communication caused by the many dialects. To solve these problems, in 1958, the Chinese Government proclaimed that a combination of the pronunciation used by the people of Beijing and other northern cities become the standard speech of China. This is called Pǔtōnghuà [普通话]—literally *common speech*—and is referred to as 'Mandarin' by Westerners. Pǔtōnghuà (also called Hànyǔ [汉语]— *the language of the Han people*) is now the language taught at school, used on TV and radio, and in all official documents.

3 The writing

Chinese is the oldest living language. It is believed that the history of Chinese writing spans over 5,000 or 6,000 years. The earliest writings discovered, dated between 1480 BC and 1122 BC, are inscribed on oracle bones and turtle shells, and are called jiǎgǔwén [甲骨文]. These writings are the records of kings in the Shang dynasty who asked the gods about their fortune for hunting, going to war or any important event.

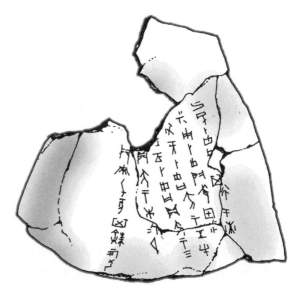

Some Chinese writing was developed from simple pictures taken from nature, such as animals, birds, mountains and rivers. The style of writing was changed several times and gradually transformed into the characters used today.

	sun	moon	mountain	tree	water	fire	person	mouth
picture	☼							
early writing	⊙							
seal form	日		山					
modern form	日	月	山	木	水	火	人	口
Pinyin	rì	yuè	shān	mù	shuǐ	huǒ	rén	kǒu

Each Chinese character is pronounced as a single syllable and has its own meanings. Many ideas, thoughts and feelings are expressed by combining two or more simple characters to form a new character with a new meaning.

日 sun	+	月 moon	=	明 bright (míng)
木 tree	+	木 tree	=	林 forest (lín)
火 fire	+	火 fire	=	炎 hot (yán)

Two or more characters can also be used together to form a further meaning, but they remain separate characters.

火 fire	followed by	山 mountain	forms	火山 volcano (huǒshān)
山 mountain	followed by	水 water	forms	山水 scenery (shānshuǐ)
口 mouth	followed by	水 water	forms	口水 saliva (kǒushuǐ)
人 people	followed by	口 mouth	forms	人口 population (rénkǒu)

4

As Chinese writing is pictographic, some characters are complicated. In 1956, the Chinese Government began simplifying the structure of some characters to make them easier to write.

dragon	traditional	龍	>	simplified	龙	(lóng)
to study	traditional	學	>	simplified	学	(xué)
country	traditional	國	>	simplified	国	(guó)
happy	traditional	歡	>	simplified	欢	(huān)

These simplified characters have been widely and officially used in China ever since. Students learn the simplified form at school and all publications in China use the simplified form; it is also the style used in this book. However, most people in overseas Chinese communities and the people of Taiwan still use the traditional style.

The principles of writing a Chinese character are basically from left to right, top to bottom, a tick and a hook. The character yǒng [永] (forever) is a good example to show the writing structure as it has many of the typical strokes used in most Chinese characters. Writing the strokes in the correct way, and in the correct order, is the first step to writing Chinese successfully.

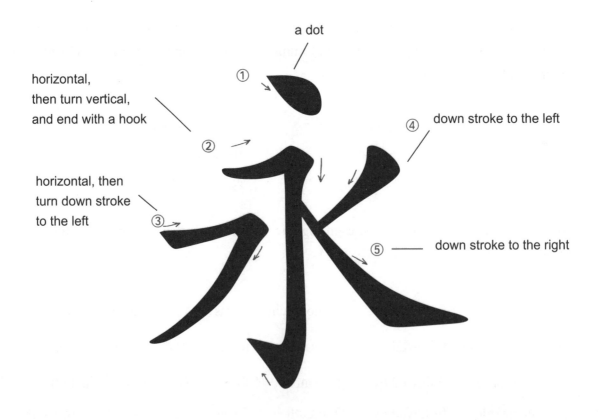

a dot

①

horizontal,
then turn vertical,
and end with a hook

②

④ down stroke to the left

horizontal, then
turn down stroke
to the left

③

⑤ down stroke to the right

Chinese books are traditionally written from top to bottom, right to left, and bound with the spine on the right-hand side. In China today, publications, except calligraphy which still follows this tradition, are usually printed in the style used in the West. However, in Taiwan most newspapers, literary works and many other publications are still presented in the traditional style.

4 Pronunciation

As Chinese had no symbols to represent the sound of the words, in 1918 the Government of the Republic of China proclaimed thirty-nine symbols to represent the sounds. These phonetic symbols, i.e. ㄅㄆㄇㄈ... were named zhùyīn fúhào [注音符号] in 1930 and thirty-seven of them are still in use in Taiwan and many Chinese communities overseas. As these symbols are not easy to learn, Westerners have adopted various ways of using Roman letters, such as the Wade-Giles system and the Yale system, to represent each Chinese sound. In 1958, the Government of the People's Republic of China introduced another Romanisation system, called *Pinyin* [pīnyīn 拼音]. Pinyin is now used in China and is an international system to express the sounds of the Chinese language as well as to spell Chinese names and places. The Pinyin system contains:

Initials		b	p	m	f		d	t	n	l
		g	k	h			j	q	x	
		zh	ch	sh	r		z	c	s	
		(y)	(w)							
Vowels	single	a	o	e	i	u	ü			
	double	ai	ei	ui	ao	ou	iu	ie	üe	er
	nasal	an	en	in	un	ün				
		ang	eng	ing	ong					
Special sounds		zhi	chi	shi	ri	zi	ci	si		
		yi	wu	yu						
		ye	yue	yin						
		yun	yuan	ying						

The pronunciation of the letters in the Pinyin system is somewhat different from that of English. Modern Chinese has 430 sounds, far less than the number of characters, therefore many characters share the same sound. The use of tone (pitch) is an important way to tell the differences in meaning of the same sound. There are four tones in the Chinese language.

—	1st tone:	high level pitch
╱	2nd tone:	rising in pitch
∨	3rd tone:	low dipping pitch
╲	4th tone:	abrupt falling in pitch

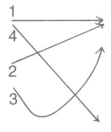

A change of tone will change the meaning of a sound. For example:

妈 mā　means　mother　　　八 bā　means　eight

麻 má　means　flax　　　　拔 bá　means　to pull

马 mǎ　means　horse　　　靶 bǎ　means　target

骂 mà　means　to scold　　爸 bà　means　father

Many characters with different meanings also share the same sound and the same tone. For example:

梅 méi—plum　　　　眉 méi—eyebrow　　　　煤 méi—coal

In addition to the four tones there is a neutral tone that does not carry any tone mark. Sometimes the second character of a two-character word uses a neutral tone. Some words that have only grammatical function also use a neutral tone. For example:

爸爸 bàba—father　　妈妈 māma—mother　　朋友 péngyou—friend

好吗？ Hǎo ma?—OK?　好啊。 Hǎo a.—OK.　太好了！ Tài hǎo le!—Great!

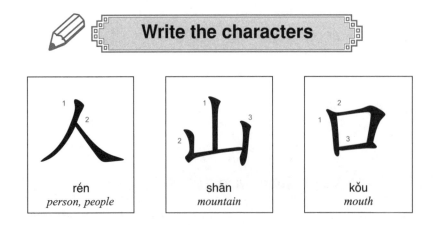

Write the characters

人　rén　*person, people*

山　shān　*mountain*

口　kǒu　*mouth*

dì èr kè nǐ hǎo
第二课 你好

1 **Hello!**

2 I am Lanlan

tóngxuémen
同学们好。

Lín lǎoshī
林老师好。

nǐ shì
你是……？

Lǐ Lánlan
我是李兰兰。
tā Bái Dàwěi
他是白大伟。

tóngxuémen zàijiàn
同学们再见。

lǎoshī zàijiàn
老师再见。

3 Good morning

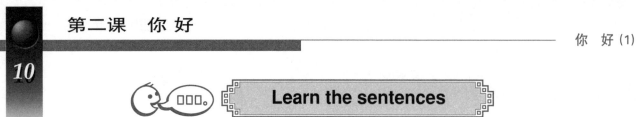

Learn the sentences

In this section you will learn to use sentences. Have a conversation with your partner to practise the sentence patterns.

Greeting people

The most common way to greet people is to say nǐ hǎo 你好, or if it is early in the morning, zǎo 早. Chinese people often say nǐ hǎo 你好 to each other at any time of the day or when they are introduced to each other.

nǐ hǎo 你 好 。	nǐ hǎo 你 好 。
Lánlan 兰 兰 ， 你 好 。	Dàwěi 大 伟 ， 你 好 。
lǎoshī 老 师 好 。	nǐmen 你 们 好 。
zǎo 早 。	zǎo 早 。
Lánlan zǎo 兰 兰 早 。	Dàwěi zǎo 大 伟 早 。

Introducing

To introduce yourself, or to state someone's name, the verb shì 是 is used whether the subject is wǒ 我, nǐ 你 or tā 他.

nǐ shì 你 是 …… ？	wǒ shì Lǐ Lánlan 我 是 李 兰 兰 。
	Lín lǎoshī 我 是 林 老 师 。
tā 他 是 …… ？	tā Bái Dàwěi 他 是 白 大 伟 。
	tā Lǐ lǎoshī 他 是 李 老 师 。

Saying goodbye

To say goodbye, say zàijiàn 再见. To say see you tomorrow, say míngtiān jiàn 明天见. The person's name or title can also be said before or after zàijiàn 再见 or míngtiān jiàn 明天见.

zàijiàn 再 见 。 míngtiān jiàn 明 天 见 。 tóngxuémen zàijiàn 同 学 们 再 见 。 míngtiān jiàn Lánlan 明 天 见 ， 兰 兰 。	zàijiàn 再 见 。 míngtiān jiàn 明 天 见 。 lǎoshī zàijiàn 老 师 再 见 。 míngtiān jiàn Dàwěi 明 天 见 ， 大 伟 。

New words and expressions

你好	nǐ hǎo	hello, how do you do
你	nǐ	you (singular)
好	hǎo	good, well
我	wǒ	I, me
是	shì	am, is, are
白	Bái	a family name bái- white
大伟	Dàwěi	Chinese for David dà- big; wěi- great
李	Lǐ	a family name lǐ- plum
兰兰	Lánlan	a Chinese given name lán- orchid
再见	zàijiàn	goodbye zài- again; jiàn- to see
同学	tóngxué	fellow student, schoolmate tóng- same, together; xué- to learn
们	men	[used after a pronoun or a noun associated with people to show plural i.e. wǒmen 我们 – we; tāmen 他们 – they]
同学们	tóngxuémen	fellow students (plural of tóngxué 同学)
林	Lín	a family name lín- forest
老师	lǎoshī	teacher lǎo- old; shī- teacher
他	tā	he, him
早	zǎo	morning, early
你们	nǐmen	you (plural)
明天	míngtiān	tomorrow míng- tomorrow, bright; tiān- day
见	jiàn	to see

✏️ Write the characters

你
nǐ
you

好
hǎo
good

我
wǒ
I, me

是
shì
am, is, are

他
tā
he, him

们
men
(grammatical word)

The character 们 contains elements of a standing person 亻 and a door 门. The standing person represents its meaning and the door (mén) represents its sound. 们 is used after a pronoun or a noun associated with people to indicate plural:

Singular		Plural
我	→	我们
你	→	你们
他	→	他们
同学	→	同学们

Something about characters

The Chinese consider a woman bearing a child (especially a son) to be good. The character 好 hǎo (good) in one of the early forms was written as , which is a combination of a kneeling woman 㚢 and a child 子.

We have a son.

好! 好!

Supplementary words and expressions

Classroom phrases

请进	qǐng jìn	come in please
请坐	qǐng zuò	sit down please
站起来	zhàn qǐlai	stand up
不要说话	bú yào shuōhuà	do not talk
注意听	zhùyì tīng	listen carefully
请安静	qǐng ānjìng	quiet please
看黑板	kàn hēibǎn	look at the blackboard
把书打开	bǎ shū dǎkāi	open (your) book
到前面来	dào qiánmian lái	come to the front
请回座位	qǐng huí zuòwèi	return to (your) seat please
请坐好	qǐng zuò hǎo	sit properly please
请举手	qǐng jǔshǒu	please raise (your) hand
把手放下	bǎ shǒu fàng xià	put down (your) hand
大声点儿	dà shēng diǎnr	a little louder
再说一次	zài shuō yí cì	say (it) again
很好	hěn hǎo	very good
非常好	fēicháng hǎo	extremely good

Something to know

Greetings

Nǐ hǎo 你好 is the most common greeting used by the Chinese. It is used at any time of the day or when people are introduced to each other. Other expressions used are:

Nǐ máng ma? [你忙吗？]　　Are you busy?

Zěnmeyàng? [怎么样？]　　How is everything?

Shàng nǎr qù? [上哪儿去？]　　Where are you going?

Chī fàn le ma? [吃饭了吗？]　　Have you eaten?

These greetings show concern for each other. When asked where they are going, people do not feel that their private lives have been intruded upon and would happily answer 'going shopping', 'going to work', or other similar expressions.

Chinese names

In Chinese, the family name is placed first followed by the given name. Most names contain three characters: the first character is the family name and the following two are the given name. However, some people may have two characters for their family name or just one character for their given name.

When naming a newborn, most parents would choose Chinese characters that best express their expectations for that child, for example, Jiànxióng [健雄] (strong and brave), and Fāngfang [芳芳] (fragrant).

Addressing teachers

Chinese students do not address their teachers as Mr, Mrs, Ms or Miss, instead they use their professional title, lǎoshī [老师] (teacher). They either address their teachers as lǎoshī, or say the family name followed by lǎoshī. For example, if the teacher's family name is Lín [林], they address him/her as Lín lǎoshī [林老师]; if the teacher's family name is Bái [白], they address him/her as Bái lǎoshī [白老师].

dì sān kè yī èr sān
第 三 课 一 二 三

1 Numbers up to 10

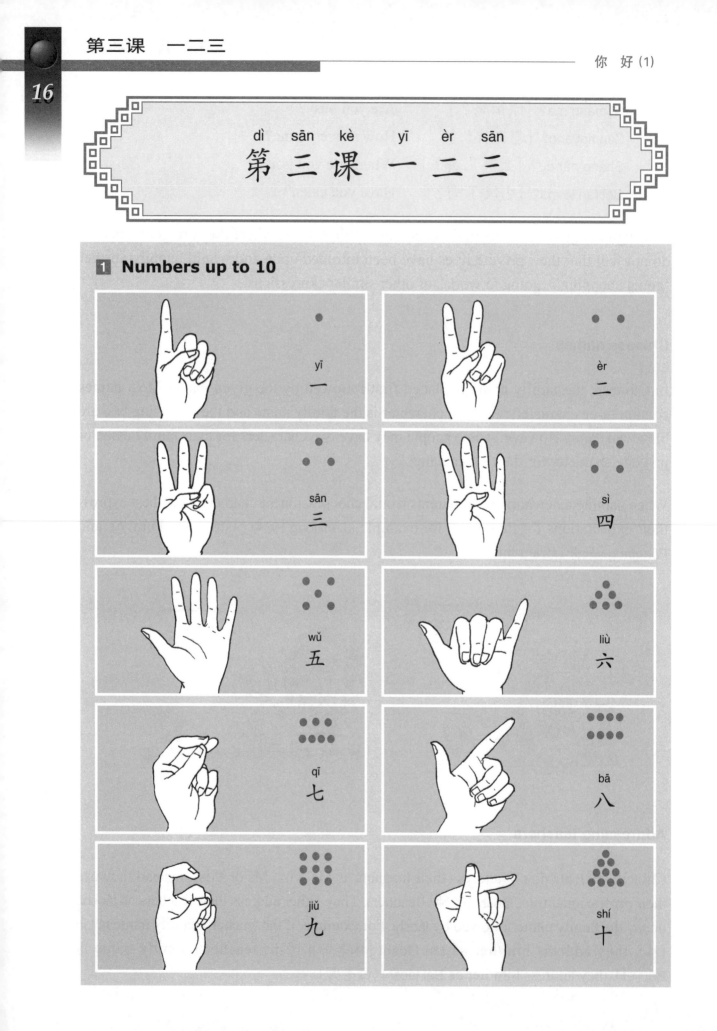

yī
一

èr
二

sān
三

sì
四

wǔ
五

liù
六

qī
七

bā
八

jiǔ
九

shí
十

一 二 三

adapted from 〈小牧童〉

一 二 三 四 五， 六 七 八 九 十；

一 二 三 四 五， 六 七 八 九 十。

lǎo shī
老 师 好。

tóng xué men
同 学 们 好。

你 好，你 好，你 好；

zài jiàn zài jiàn
再 见，再 见。

líng
○ = zero

一九○五 = 1905

二○○一 = 2001

A tongue twister

三是三，山是山；
四是四，十是十。

2 Important numbers

3 Numbers 0 to 100

líng	shí	èrshí	sānshí	sìshí
○	十	二十	三十	四十
一	十一	二十一	三十一	四十一
二	十二	二十二	三十二	四十二
三	十三	二十三	三十三	四十三
四	十四	二十四	三十四	四十四
五	十五	二十五	三十五	四十五
六	十六	二十六	三十六	四十六
七	十七	二十七	三十七	四十七
八	十八	二十八	三十八	四十八
九	十九	二十九	三十九	四十九

一三五〇七

wǔshí	liùshí	qīshí	bāshí	jiǔshí	yìbǎi
五十	六十	七十	八十	九十	一百
五十一	六十一	七十一	八十一	九十一	
五十二	六十二	七十二	八十二	九十二	
五十三	六十三	七十三	八十三	九十三	
五十四	六十四	七十四	八十四	九十四	
五十五	六十五	七十五	八十五	九十五	
五十六	六十六	七十六	八十六	九十六	
五十七	六十七	七十七	八十七	九十七	
五十八	六十八	七十八	八十八	九十八	
五十九	六十九	七十九	八十九	九十九	

4 **Maths quiz**

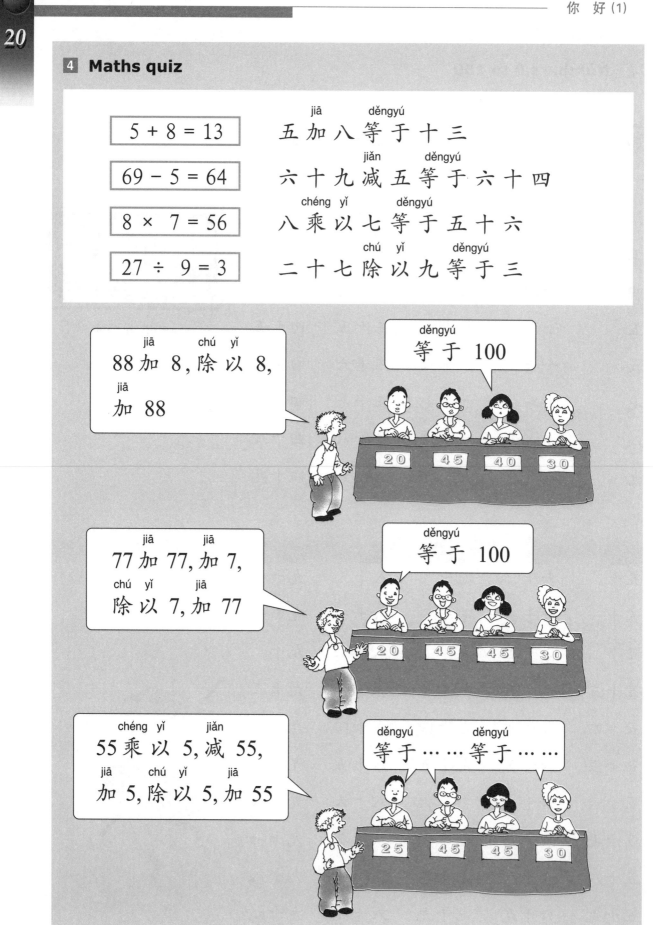

$$5 + 8 = 13$$

五加八等于十三

$$69 - 5 = 64$$

六十九减五等于六十四

$$8 × 7 = 56$$

八乘以七等于五十六

$$27 ÷ 9 = 3$$

二十七除以九等于三

88加 8，除以 8，加 88

等于 100

77加 77，加 7，除以 7，加 77

等于 100

55乘以 5，减 55，加 5，除以 5，加 55

等于⋯⋯等于⋯⋯

New words and expressions

一	yī	one		十	shí	ten
二	èr	two		○	líng	zero
三	sān	three		百	bǎi	hundred
四	sì	four		加	jiā	plus, to add
五	wǔ	five		等于	děngyú	to be equal to
六	liù	six		减	jiǎn	minus, to subtract
七	qī	seven		乘以	chéng yǐ	multiplied by
八	bā	eight				chéng- to multiply
九	jiǔ	nine		除以	chú yǐ	divided by chú- to divide

Supplementary words

Number Sequence

第一	dì yī	the first		第一课	dì yī kè	lesson one
第二	dì èr	the second		第二课	dì èr kè	lesson two
第三	dì sān	the third		第三课	dì sān kè	lesson three
……				……		

Write the characters

一	二	三	四	五
yī *one*	èr *two*	sān *three*	sì *four*	wǔ *five*

六	七	八	九	十
liù *six*	qī *seven*	bā *eight*	jiǔ *nine*	shí *ten*

Something to know

Lucky and unlucky numbers

The Chinese like the concept of pairs, believing them auspicious for happy events. The symbol [囍] (shuāng xǐ, double happiness), is formed by joining two [喜] (xǐ, happiness), and is used during wedding ceremonies to wish couples happiness for the future.

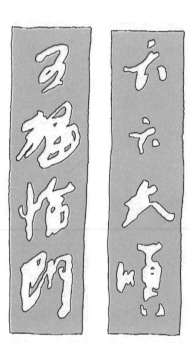

Five and six are also regarded as lucky numbers by Chinese, and are often used in phrases meaning lucky.

> wǔ fú lín mén [五福临门]   (the arrival of five happinesses)
> liù liù dà shùn [六六大顺]   (double lucky six)

Some people like to choose telephone numbers ending with double six hoping that it will bring them luck.

The number four—sì [四]—is generally regarded to be unlucky as it has the same pronunciation, although a different tone, as the word for death—sǐ [死].

People try to avoid using the number four for things associated with illness or danger. Some hospitals in Taiwan do not have a fourth floor as it would shock the patients' families to hear that their loved ones were on the 'death floor'. Some people also avoid car registration numbers ending in four. However, not all Chinese believe in this superstition, just as not all Westerners believe that the number thirteen is unlucky.

第四课 他是谁

1 Who is he?

2 Who is it?

3 How old are you?

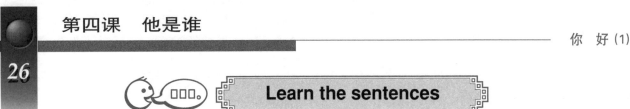

Learn the sentences

Identifying people

To ask Who is he/she? say Tā shì shéi? 他/她是谁？To answer the question, replace the question word shéi 谁 with the person's name. Note that the word order remains the same in both the question and the answer.

shéi 他 是 谁 ？	Dàwěi 他 是 大 伟 。 Mǎkè 他 是 马 克 。
她 是 谁 ？	Lín　　lǎoshī 她 是 林 老 师 。
你 是 谁 ？	Lánlan 我 是 兰 兰 。

To find out who is at the door, Chinese often say Shéi a? 谁啊？To answer this question, say Shì wǒ. 是我。or to be more polite, say your name.

a 谁 啊 ？	是 我 。 Lánlan 是 我 ， 兰 兰 。 Bái　　Dàwěi 是 我 ， 白 大 伟 。

Asking about age

To ask a child How old are you? Chinese often say Nǐ jǐ suì? 你几岁？To answer this question, replace jǐ 几 with the age. The word order remains the same whether it is a question or an answer.

It is common in Chinese to add the word jīnnián 今年 to ask how old a person is this year, so people generally ask Nǐ jīnnián jǐ suì? 你今年几岁？Note that jīnnián 今年 is not placed at the end of the sentence as this year is in English.

你 几 岁 ？ (suì)	我 八 岁 。 (suì)
他 几 岁 ？	他 三 岁 。
她 几 岁 ？	她 七 岁 。
你 今 年 几 岁 ？ (jīnnián)	我 今 年 十 一 岁 。 (jīnnián)
他 今 年 几 岁 ？	他 今 年 两 岁 。 (liǎng)

New words and expressions

谁	shéi	who, whom (a question word)
马克	Mǎkè	Chinese for Mark mǎ- horse; kè- to overcome
她	tā	she, her
啊	a	(an exclamation)
欢迎	huānyíng	welcome
请进	qǐng jìn	come in please qǐng- please; jìn- to come in
谢谢	xièxie	thanks
祝	zhù	to wish (offer good wishes)
生日	shēngrì	birthday shēng- to give birth to; rì- day, sun
快乐	kuàilè	happy kuài- happy, fast; lè- happy
今年	jīnnián	this year jīn- this, today; nián- year
几	jǐ	how many
岁	suì	year of age
两	liǎng	two (before measure words, age and some numerals)

✏️ Write the characters

谁	她	老	师	几
shéi	tā	lǎo	shī	jǐ
who, whom	*she, her*	*old*	*teacher*	*how many*

岁	两
suì	liǎng
year of age	*two*

tóngxué men　　　　　Bái　　　jīnnián
同学们好！我是白老师，今年四岁。
　　Lín
他是林老师，今年五岁。
Lǐ
李三山，你几岁？

Play school

我两岁。

Something about characters

Each Chinese character contains a basic element relating to the meaning of the character. This element is called the *'radical'*. Some characters only contain one element, that is, they are themselves radicals, such as 人 rén (people) and 山 shān (mountain). A great proportion of characters contain two elements with the radical indicating the meaning and the other element indicating the sound. For example, the character 他 tā (he), contains the radical for person 亻 and the character 她 tā (she), has the radical for woman 女. An old pronunciation of 也 in each character indicates the sound.

Something to know

Chinese age

The Chinese use two methods of counting age: one is called shísuì [实岁]—full age; and the other is called xūsuì [虚岁]—function age. Generally, people use the xūsuì method. With this method children are considered to be one year old as soon as they are born, and two years old after New Year's Eve (Chinese lunar calendar). For example, a child born on New Year's Eve would be two years old on New Year's Day.

How old are you?

Nǐ jǐ suì? [你几岁？] is the most common way to ask a child his/her age. Sometimes the Chinese also use Nǐ duō dà? [你多大？].

In Western society, adults—especially women—do not like being asked about their age, and it is considered impolite to ask an adult's age. In Chinese society, it is common for adults to ask each other's age and this is not regarded as improper. However, they do not normally ask the other's age directly, but ask the year in which he/she was born and then work out the age for themselves. The questions asked are:

Nǐ shì nǎ nián shēng de? [你是哪年生的？] In which year were you born?
Nǐ shǔ shénme? [你属什么？] In what animal year were you born?

Many elderly Chinese enjoy being asked their age as they believe it shows the questioner's respect for their experience, knowledge and health. People normally use questions such as:

Nín duō dà niánjì? [您多大年纪？] (literally—*How big is your age?*)
Nín gāo shòu? [您高寿？] (literally—*Your high age?*)

Nín [您] is the polite form of nǐ [你]. Older people, who are usually very proud of their age, would be happy to tell the questioner how old they are.

Birthdays

In the past, it was uncommon for the Chinese to celebrate their children's birthdays every year. However, due to the influence of Western ideas, some parents have begun to celebrate their children's birthdays with a birthday cake.

Traditionally, the Chinese celebrate the birth of their children—especially their sons—after the first month, and after the first year. Boiled eggs coloured red are given to friends and relatives when the baby is one month old, and a party is held when the baby is one year old. Children's birthdays are then normally ignored.

After the first birthday, the next important birthday celebration is at thirty years old and then at forty, fifty, sixty and so on. The older the person becomes, the bigger the celebration. The word shòu [寿] (longevity) is used in a variety of styles at such celebrations to wish the person a long life.

During the birthday party, steamed buns in the shape of a peach, which symbolise long life, called shòutáo [寿桃], are distributed. Noodles that also symbolise long life, called shòumiàn [寿面], are eaten. In Taiwan, guests are offered boiled pig's leg with noodles, called zhūjiǎo miànxiàn [猪脚面线]. When eating the noodles, which are usually long, the guests should be careful not to break the noodles as they represent the long life of the person celebrating his/her birthday.

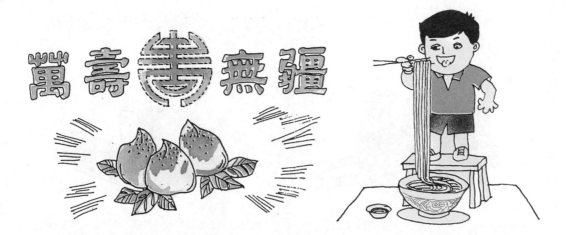

dì   wǔ   kè   zhè   shì   shéi   de
第 五 课 这 是 谁 的

1 Things I use

chǐ
尺

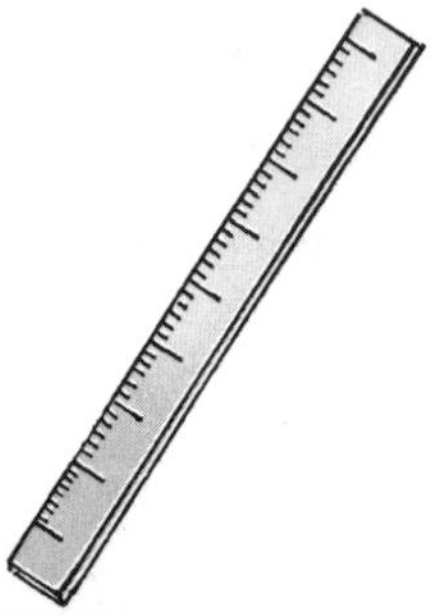

jiǎndāo
剪刀

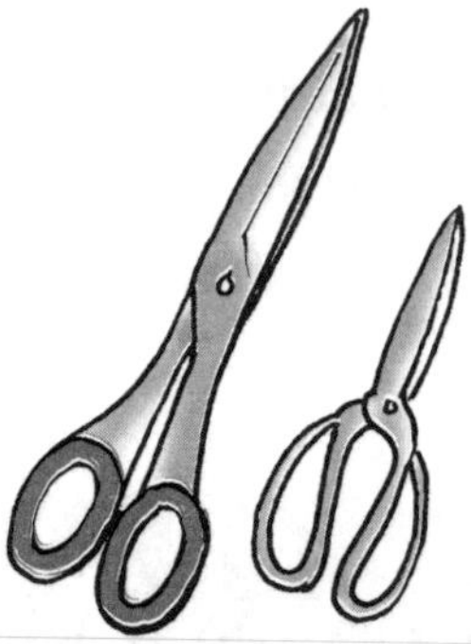

bǐ
笔

shū
书

máobǐ
毛笔

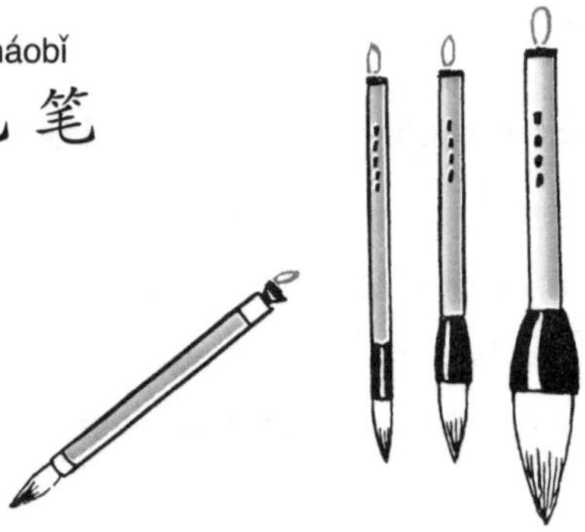

shūbāo
书包

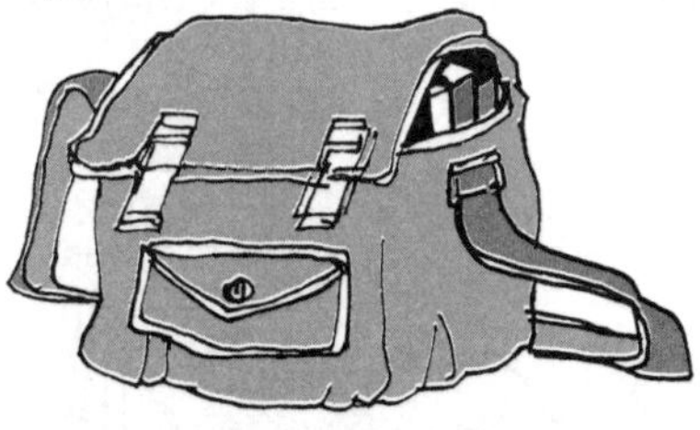

xiàngpí
橡皮

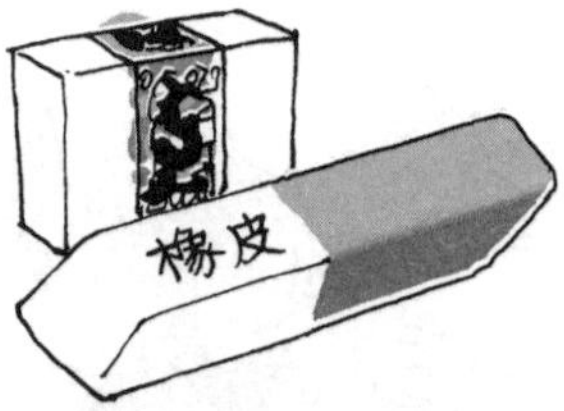

2 What is this?

3 Whose is this?

4 **Is this yours?**

Mǎkè shūbāo ma
马 克 ，这 是 你 的 书 包 吗 ？

bú nà bú
不 是 ，那 不 是 我 的 。

Dàwěi shūbāo ma
大 伟 ，这 是 你 的 书 包 吗 ？

dàgài Xiǎomíng
不 是 ，大 概 是 小 明 的 。

Xiǎomíng ma
小 明 ，这 是 你 的 吗 ？

xièxie
是 的 ，那 是 我 的 。 谢 谢 。

bú kèqi
不 客 气 。

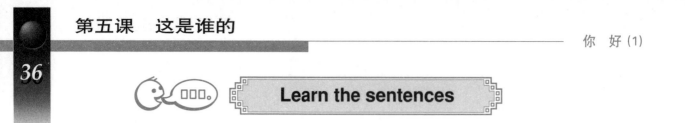

Learn the sentences

Identifying objects

To ask What is this? say Zhè shì shénme? 这是什么？ To answer the question, replace the question word shénme 什么 with the object.

zhè　　shénme 这 是 什 么 ？ nà　　shénme 那 是 什 么 ？	jiǎndāo 这 是 剪 刀 。 xiàngpí 这 是 橡 皮 。 chǐ 那 是 尺 。 máobǐ 那 是 毛 笔 。

Asking who owns an object

To ask Whose is this? say Zhè shì shéi de? 这是谁的？ To answer the question, replace the question word shéi 谁 with the owner.

de 这 是 谁 的 ？ 那 是 谁 的 ？ shū 这 是 谁 的 书 ？ bǐ 那 是 谁 的 笔 ？	de 这 是 我 的 。 Lánlan 那 是 兰 兰 的 。 shū 这 是 老 师 的 书 。 Dàwěi 这 是 大 伟 的 。 Xiǎomíng　　bǐ 那 是 小 明 的 笔 。 那 是 我 的 。

Asking if things belong to someone

To say This is your book. say Zhè shì nǐ de shū. 这是你的书。To ask Is this your book? say Zhè shì nǐ de shū ma? 这是你的书吗？

The first statement was changed into a question by adding the question word ma 吗 at the end. This is one way to turn a statement into a question where the answer can be yes or no.

Chinese answer yes to a question by repeating the verb and answer no by saying the negative form of the verb used in the question. The negative form of shì 是 is búshì 不是. For yes, shìde 是的 is sometimes used instead of shì 是, as it sounds better.

这是你的书包吗？ *shūbāo ma*	是，这是我的。 不是，这不是我的。 *bú bú*
那是你的毛笔吗？ *máobǐ*	是的，那是我的。 不是，那不是我的。 *bú*

Asking if someone knows something

To ask Do you know? say Nǐ zhīdao ma? 你知道吗？ To answer yes, repeat the verb in the question, i.e. zhīdao 知道. To answer no, add the negative word bù 不 in front of the verb, i.e. bù zhīdao 不知道.

你知道吗？ *zhīdao*	我知道。 *zhīdao* 我不知道。
他知道吗？	他知道。 他不知道。

🔑 New words and expressions

谁的	shéi de	whose	shéi- who
尺	chǐ	ruler	
剪刀	jiǎndāo	scissors	jiǎn- to cut; dāo- knife
笔	bǐ	pen	
书	shū	book	
毛笔	máobǐ	writing brush	máo- fur, feather, wool; bǐ- pen
书包	shūbāo	school bag	shū- book; bāo- bag
橡皮	xiàngpí	eraser	xiàng- rubber tree; pí- skin, leather
这	zhè	this	
什么	shénme	what	
不	bù	no, not (used to form negative) —tone changes to second when followed by a fourth tone, e.g. bú shì 不是	
知道	zhīdao	to know	
吗	ma	(a question word)	
那	nà	that	
的	de	(a possessive particle used after the pronoun or noun)	
我的	wǒ de	my, mine	
大概	dàgài	probably	dà- big; gài- approximate
你的	nǐ de	your, yours	
不是	bú shì	no (negative form of shì 是)	
小明	Xiǎomíng	a Chinese given name	xiǎo- small, little; míng- bright
是的	shìde	yes (positive answer to questions using the verb shì 是)	
不客气	bú kèqi	not at all, don't mention it, you're welcome	bù, bú- no, not; kèqi- polite
和	hé	and	

Supplementary words

Nouns for students

教室	jiàoshì	classroom	椅子	yǐzi	chair
门	mén	door	铅笔	qiānbǐ	pencil
窗户	chuānghu	window	铅笔盒	qiānbǐhé	pencil case
黑板	hēibǎn	blackboard	圆珠笔	yuánzhūbǐ	biro, ball-point pen
黑板擦	hēibǎncā	blackboard duster	胶水	jiāoshuǐ	glue
粉笔	fěnbǐ	chalk	彩笔	cǎibǐ	colour pencil
桌子	zhuōzi	desk	纸	zhǐ	paper

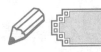

Write the characters

这 zhè *this*

那 nà *that*

什 shén *what*

么 me *(word ending)*

吗 ma *(question word)*

的 de *(possessive particle)*

不 bù *not*

'Found and Lost'

1

2

3

4

5

6

A rhyme

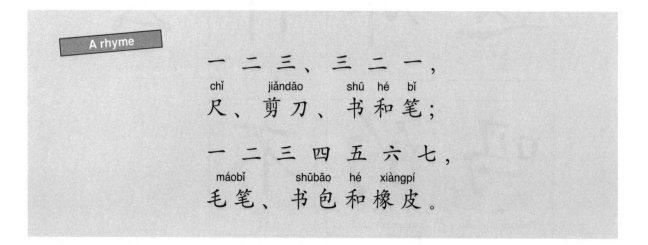

一 二 三 、 三 二 一 ，

chǐ　jiǎndāo　shū hé bǐ
尺 、 剪 刀 、 书 和 笔 ；

一 二 三 四 五 六 七 ，

máobǐ　shūbāo hé xiàngpí
毛 笔 、 书 包 和 橡 皮 。

Something to know

The finger-guessing game

Chinese children often use 'finger-guessing' to decide what game to play or who will be the first player in a game. This finger-guessing game is called cāiquán [猜拳]—guess the fist. The players thrust out a hand in one of three ways: scissors, stone or cloth. Jiǎndāo [剪刀] (scissors) is formed by extending and separating the index and middle fingers. Shítou [石头] (stone) is formed by making a fist and bù [布] (cloth) is formed by an open hand. The winner is:

scissors	cut	cloth	=	scissors win
cloth	wraps	stone	=	cloth wins
stone	breaks	scissors	=	stone wins

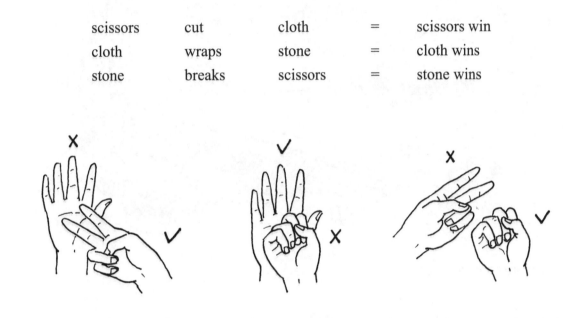

When playing the finger-guessing game, the players usually chant jiǎndāo 剪刀、shítou 石头、bù 布 and thrust out their hands, or alternatively say 一、二、三.

Calligraphy

Shūfǎ [书法] (calligraphy) is a Chinese art. Most Chinese artists are skilled in both calligraphy and painting as they are related art forms. The Chinese believe that an artist should be a master of the brush and should be able to write well.

The four traditional tools for calligraphy are the máobǐ [毛笔] (brush), the mò [墨] (ink-stick), the zhǐ [纸] (paper), and the yàntái [砚台] (ink-stone). The ink-stick is ground on the ink-stone with a little water to make ink. To save time, many people nowadays use bottled ink instead. Good calligraphy is treasured as much as a good painting. People frame and hang calligraphy on their walls to appreciate and admire it as they would a painting.

Early Chinese inventions

Paper, gunpowder and the compass are the three most commonly known Chinese inventions. Chinese first used silk floss then linen pulp to make paper. In 105 AD, Cai Lun further improved the technique by pounding bark, linen scraps and old fish nets into a pulp which was spread to form paper. This 'Cai Lun' paper was then popularly used. Gunpowder was invented by Chinese between 220 and 280 AD. By the 10th century, the use of gunpowder was common. However, gunpowder was first used to power rockets and firecrackers rather than for military, engineering or mining purposes. It was more than 2,000 years ago when the earth's magnetism was observed by the Chinese and a magnetised needle device was developed in the 11th century.

China has the longest history of producing silk and its exporting of silk formed 'silk roads' to the West and to northeast Asia. Bi Sheng invented moveable type for printing in the 11th century, around 400 years before Gutenberg's printing of the Latin Bible in the West. It was also recorded that Chinese used a silver-tin amalgam to fill holes in teeth over one thousand years ago.

dì liù kè wǒ de jiā
第 六 课 我 的 家

1 My family

bàba
爸爸

māma
妈妈

gēge
哥哥

jiějie
姐姐

我

mèimei
妹妹

dìdi
弟弟

我 的 家

adapted from 〈妹妹抱着洋娃娃〉

hé
我 家 有 七 个 人。我 有 爸爸 和 妈妈。

hé　　　　　　yě　　　　　hé
我 有 哥哥 和 姐姐;也 有 弟弟 和 妹妹。

2 Lanlan's family

jiā yǒu　　gè
我 家 有 三 个 人 。

这 是 我 的 爸爸 。
jīnnián
他 今 年 四 十 五 岁 。
gōngrén
他 是 工 人 。

这 是 我 妈妈 。
jīnnián
她 今 年 三 十 八 岁 。
hùshi
她 是 护 士 。

这 是 我 。
jīnnián
我 今 年 十 二 岁 。
xuésheng
我 是 学 生 。

3 David's family

你好。

我姓白，我叫白大伟。
xìng Bái jiào Bái Dàwěi

我家有五个人。

我爸爸是医生。
yīshēng

我妈妈是老师。

我有一个哥哥，一个妹妹。

我哥哥叫保罗 (Paul)。
jiào Bǎoluó

我妹妹叫丽丽 (Lily)。
jiào Lìlì

4 **Do you have any brothers or sisters?**

Learn the sentences

Asking about family

English sometimes uses words to state the number of things, for example, a piece of paper, a loaf of bread, a pair of shoes. Chinese, however, needs a measure word for everything, even people. The common measure word used for people is gè 个. To say one person, say yí gè rén 一个人.

To ask How many people are there in your family? say Nǐ jiā yǒu jǐ gè rén? 你家有几个人？To answer the question, replace jǐ 几 with the number of people.

你家有几个人？ 他家有几个人？	我家有三个人。 我家有五个人。 他家有七个人。 他家有六个人。

Stating occupation

To state someone's occupation, use the verb shì 是 followed by the occupation. To say He is a doctor. say Tā shì yīshēng. 他是医生。

他是医生。
我是学生。
我爸爸是工人。
我哥哥是老师。

Asking someone's name

To ask What is your name? say Nǐ jiào shénme míngzi? 你叫什么名字？ To tell someone your family name, say wǒ xìng 我姓 followed by your family name. To tell someone your full name or just your given name, say wǒ jiào 我叫 followed by your full name or your given name. Remember, when saying your full name, always say your family name first and then your given name.

jiào　　　míngzi 你 叫 什 么 名 字 ？	xìng Bái　　jiào Bái　Dàwěi 我 姓 白， 叫 白 大 伟。 Lǐ　　　　　Lǐ　Lánlan 我 姓 李， 叫 李 兰 兰。 Bái　Bǎoluó 我 叫 白 保 罗。 Lìli 我 叫 丽 丽。

Asking about brothers and sisters

To ask Do you have any elder brothers? say Nǐ yǒu gēge ma? 你有哥哥吗？ The same pattern is used to ask about elder sisters, younger brothers and younger sisters.

We learnt in lesson five that to answer yes to this type of question, repeat the verb, which in this example is yǒu 有. To answer no, use the negative form of the verb. The negative word used for yǒu 有 is méi 没, so the answer to this question is either yǒu 有 or méi yǒu 没有.

你 有 哥 哥 吗 ？ 你 有 妹 妹 吗 ？	有， 我 有 两 个 哥 哥。 méi 没 有， 我 没 有 哥 哥。 有， 我 有 一 个 妹 妹。 我 没 有 妹 妹。

New words and expressions

家	jiā	family, home
爸爸	bàba	dad, father
妈妈	māma	mum, mother
哥哥	gēge	elder brother
姐姐	jiějie	elder sister
弟弟	dìdi	younger brother
妹妹	mèimei	younger sister
有	yǒu	to have, there is/are
个	gè	(a common measure word which can be used for people)
也	yě	also, too
工人	gōngrén	labourer, worker gōng- work; rén- person, people
护士	hùshi	nurse hù- to nurse; shì- a person trained in a certain field
学生	xuésheng	student, pupil xué- to learn, to study; shēng- pupil, student, person
姓	xìng	family name, surname
叫	jiào	to be called, to call
医生	yīshēng	doctor yī- to cure; shēng- pupil, student, person
保罗	Bǎoluó	Chinese for Paul bǎo- to keep; luó- to collect
丽丽	Lìli	Chinese for Lily lì- beautiful
呢	ne	(a question word) how about, e.g. nǐ ne 你呢？– how about you?
		nǐ jiā ne 你家呢？– how about your family?
没	méi	(a negative word)
没有	méi yǒu	not have
名字	míngzi	name

✏️ Write the characters

家	有	个	爸	妈
jiā	yǒu	gè	bà	mā
family, home	*to have, there is/are*	*(measure word)*	*father*	*mother*

哥	姐	弟	妹
gē	jiě	dì	mèi
elder brother	*elder sister*	*younger brother*	*younger sister*

📕 Supplementary words

More about the family

爷爷	yéye	grandad, grandfather
奶奶	nǎinai	grandma, grandmother
继父	jìfù	stepfather
继母	jìmǔ	stepmother
伯伯	bóbo	father's elder brother
叔叔	shūshu	father's younger brother (pronounced as shúshu in Taiwan)
舅舅	jiùjiu	mother's brother
姑姑	gūgu	father's sister
姨	yí	mother's sister (said as āyí 阿姨 in Taiwan)
丈夫	zhàngfu	husband
妻子	qīzi	wife
先生	xiānsheng	Mr, also used as husband
太太	tàitai	Mrs, also used as wife
儿子	érzi	son
女儿	nǚ'ér	daughter

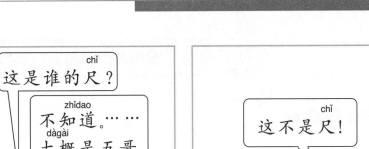

Something to know

Family size

Traditionally, the Chinese had big families. Three or four generations, including brothers' and cousins' families, usually all lived together in one large house. However, this situation has changed dramatically since the beginning of the 20th century. Small families made up of parents and their unmarried children have become more and more common.

The large family tradition was further shattered in the 1970s when the *one family, one child policy* was introduced. People used to like having many children, especially sons to carry on the family name and to help with work. The policy, aiming to reduce the population growth, was strictly practised and as a result, a great proportion of families have been down-sized to three members. Although a change to this policy in 2000 has allowed some families to have two children, it only applies to families where both husband and wife are from single child families.

Something about characters

Long ago, pigs were considered to be important family members as they represented the wealth of the family. The early form of the character 家 jiā (family or home), was written as 㝓 which is a pig 豕 under a shelter 宀.

The character 妈 mā (mother) has the radical for woman 女 nǚ, while the character 吗 ma (a question word) has the radical for mouth 口 kǒu. Both these characters take their sound, but in different tones, from the element horse 马 mǎ.

Addressing family members

In the traditional large Chinese family, a system based on respect has been developed to keep the family in harmony. Under this system, one does not call older members of the family by their given names but uses forms of address or titles instead.

The forms of address used are more complicated than those used in Western countries. The brothers of both parents are all called 'uncles' in the West. In China however, the father's elder brothers are called bóbo [伯伯] and his younger brothers are called shūshu [叔叔]. All the mother's brothers are called jiùjiu [舅舅]. Similarly, there are different forms of address for the father's sisters, the mother's sisters and the wives of the uncles—all of whom are called 'aunts' or 'aunties' in the West.

Elder brothers are called gēge [哥哥] and elder sisters are called jiějie [姐姐] by their younger siblings. If there is more than one elder brother or sister, an order title is added ahead of the address, i.e. dàgē [大哥], èrgē [二哥], sāngē [三哥], dàjiě [大姐], èrjiě [二姐], sānjiě [三姐], etc. This also applies to cousins, i.e. elder cousins are called gēge 哥哥 and jiějie 姐姐 by their younger cousins.

Some addresses are not only used among relatives, they are also commonly used among friends or even strangers. People often add the surname of an elder friend ahead of gēge 哥哥 or jiějie 姐姐 to address him/her. For example, they call an elder male friend whose surname is Lín 林 as Lín Gē 林哥, and call an elder female friend whose surname is Lǐ 李 as Lǐ Jiě 李姐. To children who are strangers, people simply call them xiǎo dìdi 小弟弟 or xiǎo mèimei 小妹妹.

这是我伯伯。　这是我叔叔。　这是我舅舅。

they are all my uncles.

dì　qī　kè　wǒ　jiā　de　chǒngwù
第 七 课 我 家 的 宠 物

1 What pets do you have?

chǒngwù
你家有什么宠物？

zhī gǒu
我家有两只狗。

pǐ mǎ
我家有四匹马。

tiáo jīnyú
我家有六条金鱼。

zhī māo
我家有五只猫。

zhī niǎo
我家有三只鸟。

2 Opposites

pǐ　　hěn dà
这匹马很大。

niǎo hěn xiǎo
那只鸟很小。

hěn xiōng
这只狗很凶。

māo　　kě'ài
这只猫很可爱。

xiōng
这个人很凶。

kě'ài
这个妹妹很可爱。

3 A cute dog

那只狗是谁的？

是我的。

你的狗真小。
zhēn

是啊！它很可爱。
a tā kě'ài

你有没有狗？

有，我有一只狗。
我的狗很大，很凶。
xiōng

Learn the sentences

Stating the number of animals

We learnt in lesson six that when stating the number of things, measure words are needed and that the measure word for people is gè 个. When counting birds, dogs or cats, use zhī 只. The measure word used for horse is pǐ 匹 and for fish tiáo 条.

我家有三只狗。
他家有两匹马。
她家有五条金鱼。

Asking about pets and family members

To ask What pets do you have? say Nǐ jiā yǒu shénme chǒngwù/dòngwù? 你家有什么宠物/动物？ To answer the question, replace shénme chǒngwù 什么宠物 with the kind of pet you have. The same sentence pattern can be used to ask What family members do you have？ Nǐ jiā yǒu shénme rén? 你家有什么人？

你家有什么宠物？	我家有六只猫。 我家有四匹马。
你家有什么动物？	我家有一只狗和两只猫。
你家有什么人？	我家有爸爸、妈妈、哥哥和我。 我家有妈妈、弟弟和我。

Describing things

Measure words are not only used between the number and the object, they are also used with the words zhè 这 and nà 那. To say this dog, say zhè zhī gǒu 这只狗.

An adjective in Chinese is used in front of the noun it qualifies, therefore to say big dog, say dà gǒu 大狗. When an adjective is used after the noun, it turns into a special kind of verb called a stative verb. Stative verbs take the place of the verb 是 shì, and normally use adverbs such as hěn 很 (very) and zhēn 真 (really) in front of them. To say This dog is very big. say Zhè zhī gǒu hěn dà. 这只狗很大。Notice that the verb shì 是 is not needed.

　　　　　　hěn
这 只 狗 很 大 。
　　　māo　　　kě'ài
这 只 猫 很 可 爱 。
　　　　　　xiōng
那 个 人 很 凶 。

Asking if someone has pets

We learnt in lessons five and six that the question word ma 吗 can be placed at the end of a statement to change it into a question. There is another way to change a statement into a question, that is to add a negative form of the verb right after the verb in the statement. There are now two verbs in the sentence: the original verb followed by the negative of the same verb. So to ask Do you have a dog? say:

Nǐ jiā yǒu gǒu <u>ma</u> ?　　or　　Nǐ jiā yǒu <u>méi yǒu</u> gǒu?
你家有狗<u>吗</u>？　　　　　　　你家有<u>没有</u>狗？

It is important to become familiar with these two ways of asking questions as they are both commonly used by the Chinese.

你家有狗吗？	有，我家有一只狗。 没有，我家没有狗。
你家有没有狗？	有，我家有两只狗。 我家没有狗。

New words and expressions

宠物	chǒngwù	pet chǒng- to spoil, to favour; wù- object, thing
只	zhī	(a measure word used for some animals, i.e. dogs, cats, birds)
狗	gǒu	dog
匹	pǐ	(a measure word used for horses, pronounced as pī in Taiwan)
马	mǎ	horse
条	tiáo	(a measure word for some long and thin objects)
金鱼	jīnyú	goldfish jīn- gold; yú- fish
猫	māo	cat
鸟	niǎo	bird
很	hěn	very
大	dà	big, large
小	xiǎo	small, little (in size)
凶	xiōng	fierce, ferocious
可爱	kě'ài	lovely kě- lovely, can, may; ài- to love
真	zhēn	really
是啊	shì a	yes, yeah (shows agreement)
它	tā	it
动物	dòngwù	animal dòng- to move; wù- object, thing
跑来跑去	pǎolái-pǎoqù	to run around pǎo- to run; lái- to come; qù- to go
它们	tāmen	they (plural of tā 它)
都	dōu	all

Something about characters

When describing something big, we often extend our arms to help our description. The early form of the character 大 dà (big) was written as 大, which has a similar appearance to a person standing with legs apart and arms extended. The early form of the character 小 xiǎo (small) was written as 小, resembling a picture of a person with his arms at his side to indicate small.

Write the characters

宠	物	只	狗	马
chǒng *to spoil*	wù *object, thing*	zhī *(measure word)*	gǒu *dog*	mǎ *horse*
很	大	小	没	
hěn *very*	dà *big*	xiǎo *little, small*	méi *(negative word)*	

Supplementary words

Living things around us

熊猫	xióngmāo	panda
袋鼠	dàishǔ	kangaroo
考拉(树熊)	kǎolā (shùxióng)	koala, called wúwěixióng 無尾熊 in Taiwan
苍蝇	cāngying	fly
蚊子	wénzi	mosquito
蚂蚁	mǎyǐ	ant
蟑螂	zhānglǎng	cockroach
蝴蝶	húdié	butterfly
蜜蜂	mìfēng	bee
鸭子	yāzi	duck
蝙蝠	biānfú	bat
鳄鱼	èyú	crocodile

我家的宠物

adapted from 〈我是只小小鸟〉

我 家 有 两 匹 马, 三 只 猫, 四 只 狗,
pǐ *mǎ* *māo*

跑 来 跑 去。 我 家 有 五 条 鱼,
pǎo *lái* *pǎo* *qù* *tiáo* *yú*

我 家 有 六 只 鸟。 它 们 都 很 可 爱。
niǎo *tā* *dōu* *kě* *ài*

A family portrait

我叫马九山。我家有四个人。我有爸爸、妈妈和一个妹妹。

我爸爸今年四十七岁。他是老师。我妈妈三十九岁。她是医生。我今年
yīshēng
十二岁，我妹妹六岁。我们都是学生。
xuésheng

我家有很多宠物。我们有三只猫，
māo
一只鸟和两只狗。猫是妈妈的，鸟
niǎo *māo* *niǎo*
是妹妹的。狗一只是爸爸的，一只是
我的。爸爸的狗很大，很凶；我的狗
xiōng
很小，很可爱。
kě'ài

The more the better?

老鼠	lǎoshǔ	rat, mouse
牛	niú	cow, ox
老虎	lǎohǔ	tiger
兔子	tùzi	rabbit, hare
龙	lóng	dragon
蛇	shé	snake, serpent
马	mǎ	horse
羊	yáng	goat, ram
猴子	hóuzi	monkey
鸡	jī	rooster, chicken
狗	gǒu	dog
猪	zhū	pig, boar

The twelve animals of the Chinese zodiac

Unlike the Western zodiac, which is a twelve-month cycle, the Chinese zodiac is a twelve-year cycle and is based on twelve animals, called shí'èr shēngxiào [十二生肖]. Each animal represents a year and the corresponding zodiac sign is thought to affect the prosperity of that year and the fate of those born that year.

People born in the year of the 'rat' are presumed to be intelligent and popular; those born in the year of the 'ox' are methodical and conscientious workers. The 'tiger' person is courageous and charismatic; the 'rabbit' is a well-mannered pacifist; the 'dragon' is ambitious and has the quality of leadership; the 'snake' has an active mind and enjoys a challenge; the 'horse' is charming and enjoys being the centre of attention; the 'goat' is creative and has an easy-going nature; the 'monkey' is imaginative and curious; the 'rooster' is flamboyant and well-read; the 'dog' is honourable and has a strong sense of fair play; the 'pig' is honest and has an understanding nature.

The rat	The ox	The tiger
1948 年 2 月 10 日 – 1949 年 1 月 28 日	1949 年 1 月 29 日 – 1950 年 2 月 16 日	1950 年 2 月 17 日 – 1951 年 2 月 5 日
1960 年 1 月 28 日 – 1961 年 2 月 14 日	1961 年 2 月 15 日 – 1962 年 2 月 4 日	1962 年 2 月 5 日 – 1963 年 1 月 24 日
1972 年 2 月 15 日 – 1973 年 2 月 2 日	1973 年 2 月 3 日 – 1974 年 1 月 22 日	1974 年 1 月 23 日 – 1975 年 2 月 10 日
1984 年 2 月 2 日 – 1985 年 2 月 19 日	1985 年 2 月 20 日 – 1986 年 2 月 8 日	1986 年 2 月 9 日 – 1987 年 1 月 28 日
1996 年 2 月 19 日 – 1997 年 2 月 7 日	1997 年 2 月 8 日 – 1998 年 1 月 27 日	1998 年 1 月 28 日 – 1999 年 2 月 15 日

The rabbit	The dragon	The snake
1951 年 2 月 6 日 – 1952 年 1 月 26 日	1952 年 1 月 27 日 – 1953 年 2 月 13 日	1953 年 2 月 14 日 – 1954 年 2 月 2 日
1963 年 1 月 25 日 – 1964 年 2 月 12 日	1964 年 2 月 13 日 – 1965 年 2 月 1 日	1965 年 2 月 2 日 – 1966 年 1 月 20 日
1975 年 2 月 11 日 – 1976 年 1 月 30 日	1976 年 1 月 31 日 – 1977 年 2 月 17 日	1977 年 2 月 18 日 – 1978 年 2 月 6 日
1987 年 1 月 29 日 – 1988 年 2 月 16 日	1988 年 2 月 17 日 – 1989 年 2 月 5 日	1989 年 2 月 6 日 – 1990 年 1 月 26 日
1999 年 2 月 16 日 – 2000 年 2 月 4 日	2000 年 2 月 5 日 – 2001 年 1 月 23 日	2001 年 1 月 24 日 – 2002 年 2 月 11 日

The horse	The goat	The monkey
1954 年 2 月 3 日 – 1955 年 1 月 23 日	1955 年 1 月 24 日 – 1956 年 2 月 11 日	1956 年 2 月 12 日 – 1957 年 1 月 30 日
1966 年 1 月 21 日 – 1967 年 2 月 8 日	1967 年 2 月 9 日 – 1968 年 1 月 29 日	1968 年 1 月 30 日 – 1969 年 2 月 16 日
1978 年 2 月 7 日 – 1979 年 1 月 27 日	1979 年 1 月 28 日 – 1980 年 2 月 15 日	1980 年 2 月 16 日 – 1981 年 2 月 4 日
1990 年 1 月 27 日 – 1991 年 2 月 14 日	1991 年 2 月 15 日 – 1992 年 2 月 3 日	1992 年 2 月 4 日 – 1993 年 1 月 22 日
2002 年 2 月 12 日 – 2003 年 1 月 31 日	2003 年 2 月 1 日 – 2004 年 1 月 21 日	2004 年 1 月 22 日 – 2005 年 2 月 8 日

The rooster	The dog	The pig
1957 年 1 月 31 日 – 1958 年 2 月 17 日	1958 年 2 月 18 日 – 1959 年 2 月 7 日	1959 年 2 月 8 日 – 1960 年 1 月 27 日
1969 年 2 月 17 日 – 1970 年 2 月 5 日	1970 年 2 月 6 日 – 1971 年 1 月 26 日	1971 年 1 月 27 日 – 1972 年 2 月 14 日
1981 年 2 月 5 日 – 1982 年 1 月 24 日	1982 年 1 月 25 日 – 1983 年 2 月 12 日	1983 年 2 月 13 日 – 1984 年 2 月 1 日
1993 年 1 月 23 日 – 1994 年 2 月 9 日	1994 年 2 月 10 日 – 1995 年 1 月 30 日	1995 年 1 月 31 日 – 1996 年 2 月 18 日

The Chinese zodiac is based on the lunar calendar, so the first day of the Chinese year is not the first of January as on the calendar we use today. The chart above will help you find your Chinese zodiac sign. Most Chinese know the sign of the animal in which they are born and fortune-tellers sometimes take it into consideration when people seek advice in choosing a wife or a husband. However this is regarded as superstitious by some people.

Why these twelve animals?

Long ago, people did not know how to count the years and so they asked the Jade Emperor, Yùhuáng Dàdì [玉皇大帝] for help. The Jade Emperor decided to hold a race through a forest and across a river on his birthday with all of the animals as competitors and decreed that each of the first twelve would have a year named after it.

At the time, the rat and the cat were good friends and so they decided to help each other. Worrying that they might sleep in, they asked the ox, who was an early riser, for help. On the morning of the race, the ox, seeing that the rat and the cat were too sleepy to get up, told them to jump on his back and he would carry them. When the ox was crossing the river, the rat woke up and realised that the cat, who was a fast runner, would certainly come first, so he pushed the cat into the river. As soon as the ox reached the river bank the rat ran as fast as he could and won the race, with the ox in second place. The tiger came third and the rabbit, who jumped across the river on the backs of the other animals, came fourth. The dragon, who was certainly the fastest but had to go to the east to make rain, came fifth. The snake and the horse came next, followed by the goat, the monkey and the rooster, who shared a tree trunk to cross the river. The dog came eleventh and finally the pig managed to make last place.

The cat finally arrived while the twelve victorious animals were celebrating. When he found that he was too late he tried to catch the rat for revenge and that is why cats, to this day, like to catch rats and mice to eat.

The giant panda

The giant panda, called dà xióngmāo [大熊猫], is a unique Chinese animal and its cuddly appearance has made it popular throughout the world. Its diet consists mainly of bamboo. To adapt to this special diet, the panda developed a special sixth digit on its paws to help it grab and hold the young bamboo shoots.

The decrease in the area of bamboo forests has caused the number of pandas to decline. In 1988, it was estimated that the number had dwindled to around 800. The Chinese Government has now established twelve reserves in the provinces of Sichuan [Sìchuān 四川], Gansu [Gānsù 甘肃] and Shaanxi [Shǎnxī 陕西]. The most popular is the Wolong reserve in Sichuan.

There is a legend about why pandas have black fur surrounding their eyes. Once, a shepherd sacrificed his life rescuing a young panda from being eaten by a leopard. The pandas held a ceremony to honour the heroic shepherd and they were so sad during the ceremony that they wept until the tears stained the fur surrounding their eyes, and the stain remains today.

dì　bā　kè　　wǒ　huì　shuō　Hànyǔ
第八课　我会说汉语

1 Countries

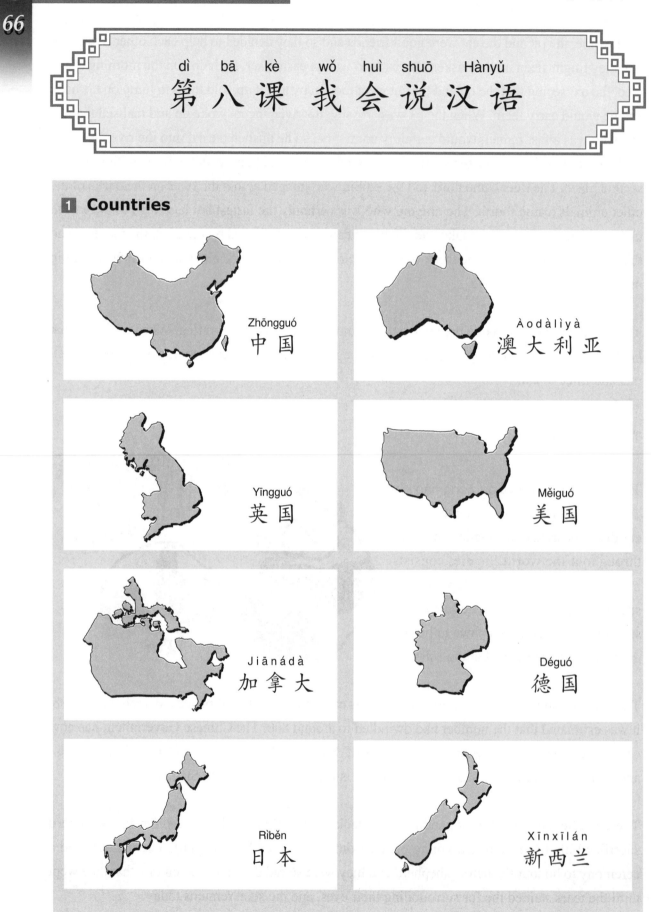

Zhōngguó
中国

Àodàlìyà
澳大利亚

Yīngguó
英国

Měiguó
美国

Jiānádà
加拿大

Déguó
德国

Rìběn
日本

Xīnxīlán
新西兰

2 Where are you from?

3 I am an Australian

4 **Can you speak Chinese?**

qǐngwèn　huì shuō Hànyǔ
请问，你会说汉语吗？

huì shuō Hànyǔ
她不会说汉语。

yí　huì shuō Hànyǔ
咦，你会说汉语？！

yìdiǎnr
我会说一点儿。

de
你说得很好。

nǎli
哪里！哪里！

Learn the sentences

Asking about someone's nationality

To state a person's nationality, simply add rén 人 after the name of the country.

澳大利亚	Àodàlìyà	>	澳大利亚人	Àodàlìyàrén	Australian
中国	Zhōngguó	>	中国人	Zhōngguórén	Chinese
美国	Měiguó	>	美国人	Měiguórén	American
英国	Yīngguó	>	英国人	Yīngguórén	British
日本	Rìběn	>	日本人	Rìběnrén	Japanese
德国	Déguó	>	德国人	Déguórén	German
加拿大	Jiānádà	>	加拿大人	Jiānádàrén	Canadian
新西兰	Xīnxīlán	>	新西兰人	Xīnxīlánrén	New Zealander

To ask a person his/her nationality, say Nǐ shì nǎ guó rén? 你是哪国人？ To answer the question, replace nǎ guó rén 哪国人 with the nationality.

nǎ guó 你是哪国人？	Àodàlìyàrén 我是澳大利亚人。
	我是中国人。
nǎ 他是哪国人？	Rìběnrén 他是日本人。
nǎ 她是哪国人？	Měiguórén 她是美国人。

Asking if someone is of a certain nationality

We learnt in lesson seven that there are two ways to ask questions that can be answered by saying yes or no; both ways can be used to ask someone if he or she is of a certain nationality. To ask *Are you Chinese?* say:

Nǐ shì Zhōngguórén <u>ma</u>?　　or　　Nǐ shì <u>bú shì</u> Zhōngguórén?

你是中国人<u>吗</u>?　　　　　　　　你是<u>不是</u>中国人?

你 是 中 国 人 吗 ？ Déguórén 他 是 德 国 人 吗 ？	ᵃ 是 啊， 我 是 中 国 人 。 不 是， 我 不 是 中 国 人 。 Déguórén 是 的， 他 是 德 国 人 。 Déguórén 他 不 是 德 国 人 。
你 是 不 是 中 国 人 ？ Yīngguórén 他 是 不 是 英 国 人 ？	是， 我 是 中 国 人 。 我 不 是 中 国 人 。 Yīngguórén 他 是 英 国 人 。 Yīngguórén 他 不 是 英 国 人 。

Asking about language ability

To ask someone if he or she can speak a certain language, again both ways of asking questions can be used.

Nǐ huì shuō Hànyǔ <u>ma</u>?　　　or　　Nǐ huì <u>bú huì</u> shuō Hànyǔ?
你会说汉语吗？　　　　　　　　　你会<u>不会</u>说汉语？

你 会 说 汉 语 吗 ？ (Hànyǔ) 他 会 说 英 语 吗 ？ (Yīngyǔ)	我 会 。 我 会 说 一 点 儿 。 (yìdiǎnr) 会 ， 他 会 说 英 语 。 (Yīngyǔ) 不 会 ， 他 不 会 说 英 语 。 (bú) (Yīngyǔ)
你 会 不 会 说 汉 语 ？ (Hànyǔ) 你 会 不 会 说 日 语 ？ (Rìyǔ) 他 会 不 会 说 德 语 ？ (Déyǔ)	我 会 说 一 点 儿 。 (yìdiǎnr) 我 不 会 说 日 语 。 (Rìyǔ) 他 会 。 他 不 会 。

Describing language ability

To say You speak very well. say Nǐ shuō de hěn hǎo. 你说得很好。 To reply Not at all, say Nǎli, nǎli. 哪里，哪里。 Chinese use de 得 after a verb to lead to the degree or result of the action of this verb, i.e. to say speak very well, say shuō de hěn hǎo 说得很好, and to say don't speak well, say shuō de bù hǎo 说得不好.

你 说 得 很 好 。 (de) 我 说 得 不 好 。	哪 里 ， 哪 里 。 (nǎli) 哪 里 ， 你 说 得 很 好 。

New words and expressions

会	huì	can, to be able to
说	shuō	to speak, to say
汉语	Hànyǔ	Chinese language Hàn- a Chinese dynasty; yǔ- language
中国	Zhōngguó	China zhōng- centre, middle; guó- country
澳大利亚	Àodàlìyà	Australia, also called Àozhōu 澳洲 in Taiwan ào- bay; dà- big; lì- sharp; yà- Asia, second; zhōu- continent
英国	Yīngguó	England (transliteration) yīng- hero
美国	Měiguó	America (transliteration), USA měi- beautiful
加拿大	Jiānádà	Canada (transliteration) jiā- to add; ná- to take; dà- big
德国	Déguó	Germany (transliteration- Deutschland) dé- virtue, morals
日本	Rìběn	Japan rì- sun, day; běn- basis, origin
新西兰	Xīnxīlán	New Zealand, called Nǐuxīlán 纽西兰 in Taiwan xīn- new; xī- west; lán- orchid; niǔ- bound
哪	nǎ	which
国	guó	country
对不起	duìbuqǐ	excuse me, sorry
没关系	méi guānxi	it doesn't matter, that's all right méi- not; guānxi- matter
请问	qǐngwèn	may I ask qǐng- please; wèn- to ask
小妹妹	xiǎomèimei	little girl
不会	bú huì	to be unable to, cannot
咦	yí	why! huh! (indicating surprise)
一点儿	yìdiǎnr	a little, a bit
得	de	(used after a verb to indicate the degree or result)
哪里	nǎli	not at all (said when praised; literally where)
英语	Yīngyǔ	English language
日语	Rìyǔ	Japanese language
德语	Déyǔ	German language

Write the characters

中
zhōng
middle

国
guó
country

澳
ào
bay

利
lì
sharp

亚
yà
second, Asia

也
yě
also, too

会
huì
can, be able to

说
shuō
to speak, to say

A personal profile

　　　　　　　　xìng　　　　　　jiào Xiǎoměi　　jīnnián
她姓山口，叫小美，今年十六岁，是
xuésheng　Xiǎoměi　　　　　　　　　　　　　　Rìběnrén
学生。小美是澳大利亚人。她爸爸是日本人，
　　　　　　　　　Xiǎoměi
妈妈是中国人。小美有一个哥哥、两个
　　　　　hé　　　　　Xiǎoměi　　Yīngyǔ　　Hànyǔ
姐姐和一个妹妹。小美会说英语、汉语
hé Rìyǔ　　　Yīngyǔ hé Hànyǔ　　de　　　Rìyǔ
和日语。她英语和汉语说得很好，日语说
de　　　　　　　　　　　　pǐ　hé　　　niǎo
得不好。小美的宠物是一匹马和一只鸟。
　　　　　　　　　　niǎo
她的马叫山山；她的鸟叫亚亚。山山很小，
　　kě'ài　　　　　　xiōng
很可爱；亚亚很大，很凶。

Something about characters

An early form of the character 中 zhōng (centre or middle) was written as 中, which looks like a vertical line through the centre or middle of a mouth. Precious jade 玉 within a boundary 口 forms 国 guó (country), indicating that all which is within the boundary of a country is precious.

Supplementary words

Countries

台湾	Táiwān	Taiwan	印度	Yìndù	India
香港	Xiānggǎng	Hong Kong	泰国	Tàiguó	Thailand
法国	Fǎguó	France	马来西亚	Mǎláixīyà	Malaysia
爱尔兰	Ài'ěrlán	Ireland	新加坡	Xīnjiāpō	Singapore
意大利	Yìdàlì	Italy	越南	Yuènán	Vietnam
希腊	Xīlà	Greece	菲律宾	Fēilǜbīn	the Philippines
新几内亚	Xīnjǐnèiyà	New Guinea	俄罗斯	Éluósī	Russia
墨西哥	Mòxīgē	Mexico	南非	Nánfēi	South Africa
瑞士	Ruìshì	Switzerland	西班牙	Xībānyá	Spain

The bird's words

它会说汉语。

它不会。

它会。

它不会说汉语；它会说英语。

它会说 "笔"。

那不是 "笔"，那是 "bee"。

它会说 "狗"。

那不是 "狗"，那是 "go"。

它会说 "你的书"。

那不是 "你的书"，那是 "Need a shoe"！

Something to know

'Mandarin' the official Chinese language

'Mandarin' is called different names by the Chinese living in different places. Since the introduction of Pinyin and simplified characters in China, there are also variations in the form of Mandarin being used. You will find that in your local Chinese community, characters used in newspapers, publications and even menus are printed in traditional characters, while publications from China are in simplified form.

Country / area	Terms	Pronunciation system	Style of character
China	Pǔtōnghuà 普通话 Hànyǔ 汉语 Zhōngwén 中文	Pinyin	simplified
Taiwan	Guóyǔ 国语 Zhōngwén 中文	Phonetic symbols (ㄅㄆㄇㄈ…)	traditional
Singapore	Huáyǔ 华语	Pinyin	simplified
Hong Kong	Zhōngwén 中文 Pǔtōnghuà 普通话	Phonetic symbols, changing to Pinyin	traditional, changing to simplified
Overseas Chinese communities	Huáyǔ 华语 Zhōngwén 中文	mainly Phonetic symbols	mainly traditional

dì jiǔ kè wǒ xǐhuān yóuyǒng
第 九 课 我 喜 欢 游 泳

1 Sports

yóuyǒng
游泳

qíchē
骑车

pǎobù
跑步

tī zúqiú
踢足球

dǎ lánqiú
打篮球

dǎ wǎngqiú
打网球

dǎ pīngpāngqiú
打乒乓球

dǎ bǎnqiú
打板球

2 What sports do you like?

3 **Let's play cricket**

喂，我们去打板球，好吗？
wèi *qù* *bǎnqiú*

好啊！我最喜欢打板球。
a *zuì* *bǎnqiú*

我不去。我最不喜欢打板球。
bú qù *zuì* *bǎnqiú*

我们走吧！
zǒu ba
再见，兰兰！
zàijiàn *Lánlan*

再见！

马克，我们去打乒乓球，好吗？
Mǎkè *qù* *pīngpāngqiú*

对不起，我不去。我很忙。
duìbuqǐ *bú* *máng*

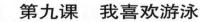

Learn the sentences

Asking what sports someone likes

To ask What sports do you like? say Nǐ xǐhuān shénme yùndòng? 你喜欢什么运动？ To answer the question, replace shénme yùndòng 什么运动 with the name of the sport.

你喜欢什么^{yùndòng}运动？	我喜欢^{yóuyǒng}游泳。 我喜欢打^{wǎngqiú}网球。 我喜欢^{qíchē}骑车。 我喜欢^{tī}踢^{zúqiú}足球。
他喜欢什么运动？	他喜欢^{pǎobù}跑步。 他喜欢打^{bǎnqiú}板球。 他喜欢^{tī}踢^{zúqiú}足球。
她喜欢什么运动？	她喜欢打^{pīngpāngqiú}乒乓球。 她喜欢打^{lánqiú}篮球。

Asking if someone likes a certain sport

To ask someone whether he/she likes a particular sport, say:

Nǐ xǐhuān... <u>ma</u>?　　　or　　　Nǐ xǐhuān <u>bù xǐhuān</u>...?
你喜欢……<u>吗</u>?　　　　　　　　你喜欢<u>不喜欢</u>……?

The expression xǐhuān bù xǐhuān 喜欢不喜欢 can be shortened to xǐ bù xǐhuān 喜不喜欢.

lánqiú 你 喜 欢 打 篮 球 吗 ? pīngpāngqiú 你 喜 欢 打 乒 乓 球 吗 ? tī　zúqiú 你 喜 不 喜 欢 踢 足 球 ? qíchē 你 喜 不 喜 欢 骑 车 ?	{ 我 喜 欢 。 { 我 不 喜 欢 。
bǎnqiú 他 喜 欢 打 板 球 吗 ? yóuyǒng 他 喜 不 喜 欢 游 泳 ?	{ 他 喜 欢 。 { 他 不 喜 欢 。

Suggesting an activity

English uses the expression Let's... to suggest an activity. In Chinese, say Wǒmen qù..., hǎo ma? 我们去……, 好吗? To answer OK. say Hǎo a! 好啊! The a 啊 is used to stress that you think it's a good idea. To answer I'm not going. say Wǒ bú qù. 我不去。

wǎngqiú 我 们 去 打 网 球 , 好 吗 ? tī　zúqiú 我 们 去 踢 足 球 , 好 吗 ? pīngpāngqiú 我 们 去 打 乒 乓 球 , 好 吗 ?	{ 好 啊 ! { 我 不 去 。

New words and expressions

喜欢	xǐhuān	to like xǐ- to like, happy; huān- happy
游泳	yóuyǒng	swimming, to swim yóu- to swim; yǒng- to swim
骑车	qíchē	1. cycling (qí zìyóuchē 骑自由车); 2. to ride a bicycle (qí zìxíngchē 骑自行车 or, in Taiwan, qí jiǎotàchē 骑脚踏车) qí- to ride on something; chē- vehicle; zìyóu- freedom, free; jiǎo- foot; tà- to tread
跑步	pǎobù	running, to jog pǎo- to run; bù- step, pace
踢	tī	to kick, to play (soccer)
足球	zúqiú	soccer zú- foot; qiú- ball
打	dǎ	to hit, to play (tennis, basketball, table tennis, etc.)
篮球	lánqiú	basketball lán- basket; qiú- ball
网球	wǎngqiú	tennis wǎng- net; qiú- ball
乒乓球	pīngpāngqiú	table tennis pīng, pāng- sound of the ball hitting the table
板球	bǎnqiú	cricket bǎn- board; qiú- ball
运动	yùndòng	sports, exercise yùn- to transport; dòng- to move
喂	wèi	hey!
去	qù	to go
好吗	hǎo ma	OK? (an expression to ask for agreement)
好啊	hǎo a	good! (agreeing)
最	zuì	most
不去	bú qù	not going (negative form of qù 去)
走	zǒu	to go, to walk
吧	ba	(expression used at the end of a sentence to indicate suggestion)
我们走吧	wǒmen zǒu ba	let's go
忙	máng	busy

Something about characters

When we are happy, we may feel like singing. The character 喜 xǐ (happy) was once written as 𠺤 which shows music 壴 coming out of a mouth 口 . The music is represented by the shape of a drum 𡴜 with decoration 㞢.

✏️ Write the characters

喜 xǐ *to like, happy*	欢 huān *happy*	运 yùn *to transport, luck*	动 dòng *to move*	打 dǎ *to hit*

球 qiú *ball*	去 qù *to go*	吧 ba *(grammatical word)*

Amazing pets

谢谢！

　　他叫林大利，今年九十四岁，是美国人。他爸爸是
中国人。林大利会说汉语，也会说一点儿日语。他有三
匹马、四只狗、两只猫、十八条金鱼和一只鸟。他的马
会踢足球；他的狗会打篮球。他的猫喜欢游泳；他的金鱼
不喜欢猫。他的鸟会说英语和汉语，它最喜欢说
"谢谢！"

Supplementary words

More Sports

橄榄球	gǎnlǎnqiú	football, rugby
棒球	bàngqiú	baseball
垒球	lěiqiú	softball
体操	tǐcāo	gymnastics
跳远	tiàoyuǎn	long jump
跳高	tiàogāo	high jump
田径	tiánjìng	track and field
保龄球	bǎolíngqiú	bowling (tenpin)
高尔夫球	gāo'ěrfūqiú	golf
排球	páiqiú	volleyball
羽毛球	yǔmáoqiú	badminton
曲棍球	qūgùnqiú	hockey

Something to know

Taijiquan

Tàijíquán 太极拳 (taichi), characterized by its graceful and slow movements, is a traditional Chinese sport and an exercise for the mind as well as the body.

To practise tàijíquán 太极拳, one needs to be relaxed and concentrate on breathing and the flow of each movement. The exercise develops physical endurance, relaxation and mental calm. It is performed by millions of Chinese daily, mainly early in the morning, in parks or anywhere else where there is enough space.

dì shí kè wǒ de péngyou
第十课 我的朋友

1 **Lanlan's friend**

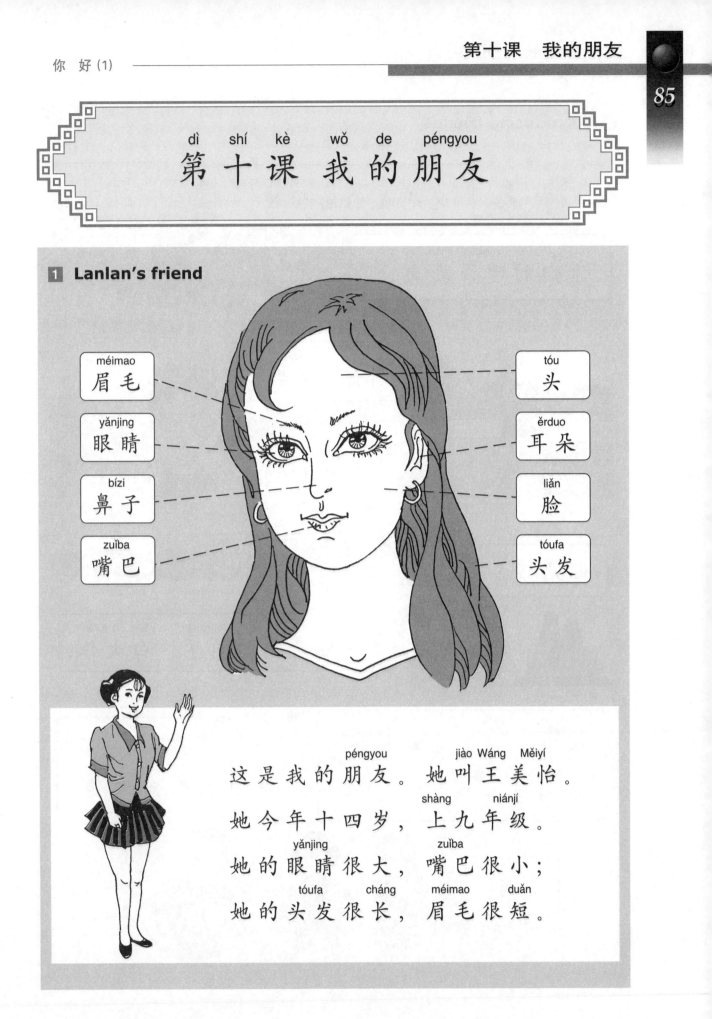

méimao
眉毛

yǎnjing
眼睛

bízi
鼻子

zuǐba
嘴巴

tóu
头

ěrduo
耳朵

liǎn
脸

tóufa
头发

péngyou
这是我的朋友。她叫王美怡。

jiào Wáng Měiyí

shàng niánjí
她今年十四岁，上九年级。

yǎnjing   zuǐba
她的眼睛很大，嘴巴很小；

tóufa   cháng   méimao   duǎn
她的头发很长，眉毛很短。

2 Introducing friends

3 What grade are you in?

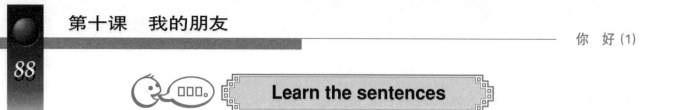

Learn the sentences

Asking what grade someone is in at school

To ask What grade are you in? say Nǐ shàng jǐ niánjí? 你上几年级？ To answer, replace the question word jǐ 几 with the grade.

你上几年级？	我上六年级。
	我上七年级。
他上几年级？	他上五年级。
	他上九年级。
她上几年级？	她上八年级。
	她上四年级。

Asking about someone's identity

We learnt in lesson four that Tā shì shéi? 他是谁？ is used to ask who a person is, and that the answer is the person's name or title. Now we'll learn to answer the question by stating the person's relationship to you or to someone else.

他是谁？	他是我的朋友。
	他是我的弟弟。
她是谁？	她是我姐姐的朋友。
	她是我妈妈。

Asking if someone is in the same class

To ask Is he in the same class as you? say Tā hé nǐ tóngbān ma? 他和你同班吗？ To answer yes, say shìde 是的; to answer no, say bù 不.

^{hé} ^{tóngbān} 他 和 你 同 班 吗？	^{tóngbān} 是 的， 他 和 我 同 班。 不， 他 不 和 我 同 班。
你 和 我 妹 妹 同 班 吗？	是 的， 我 和 她 同 班。 不， 我 不 和 她 同 班。
^{Dàwěi} 你 和 大 伟 同 班 吗？	是 的， 我 们 同 班。 不， 我 们 不 同 班。

你上几年级？一年级？

我上八年级。

A rhyme

^{cháng} ^{méi} ^{duǎn} ^{tóufa}　　^{yǎn}　^{zuǐba}
长 眉 短 头 发， 小 眼 大 嘴 巴；
^{xiàohāha}　　^{shuōhuà} ^{xiōngbāba}
打 球 笑 哈 哈， 说 话 凶 巴 巴。

New words and expressions

朋友	péngyou	friend péng- friend; yǒu- friend
眉毛	méimao	eyebrow méi- eyebrow, máo- hair
眼睛	yǎnjing	eye yǎn, jīng- eye
鼻子	bízi	nose
嘴巴	zuǐba	mouth
头	tóu	head
耳朵	ěrduo	ear ěr- ear; duǒ- measure word for flower
脸	liǎn	face
头发	tóufa	hair (on human head) tóu- head; fà- hair
王	Wáng	a family name wáng- king
美怡	Měiyí	a given name měi- beautiful; yí- happy
上	shàng	to go, to attend
年级	niánjí	grade nián- year; jí- level
长	cháng	long
短	duǎn	short
学校	xuéxiào	school xué- to learn, to study; xiào- school
同班	tóngbān	same class tóng- same; bān- class
笑哈哈	xiàohāha	to laugh heartily, laughingly xiào- to smile, to laugh
凶巴巴	xiōngbāba	fiercely, ferociously xiōng- fierece, ferocious

Write the characters

péng
friend

yǒu
friend

jiào
to be called, to call

shàng
to go, up

nián
year

jí
grade, step

hé
and

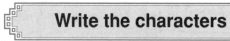

tóng
together, the same

xué
to study

My alien friends

他叫大中，是我的朋友。大中没有头发，也没有眉毛。
他有一只眼睛，两个鼻子，三个耳朵。他的眼睛很大，
鼻子和嘴巴都很小。

　　大中没有爸爸，也没有妈妈。他今年五岁，上九
年级。大中和小国同班。小国今年八岁，上四年级。他
有三只眼睛、四个鼻子、五个耳朵……。

Something about characters

The modern form of 朋 péng looks like two moons. An early form of 友 yǒu was written as 𠂢, which resembles holding hands. Both of these characters explain the foundation of friendship and are written together to mean friend.

An early form of 上 shàng was written as 丄, which represents an object standing high above the ground.

Something to know

Schools

In China, the school year begins in September with the first semester ending in mid-January. The second semester begins in February (after three weeks' vacation for the Spring Festival—Chinese New Year) and ends in mid-July, leaving six weeks for the summer vacation.

The structure of the regular education system follows a 6–3–3–4 pattern: six years of primary school [xiǎoxué 小学], three years of junior high school [chūzhōng 初中], three years of senior high school [gāozhōng 高中] and four years of tertiary education [dàxué 大学]. Entrance examinations to each higher level are very competitive. Keypoint schools, [zhòngdiǎn xuéxiào 重点学校], which are better equipped and have a higher academic standard, are the most popular schools.

In Taiwan, the school year starts in autumn and ends in summer the next year. There are two vacations: winter vacation [hánjià 寒假], around the time of the lunar New Year (end of January to beginning of February) and summer vacation [shǔjià 暑假], from July to late August. The general school system also follows a 6–3–3–4 pattern. Entrance examinations to senior high schools [gāozhōng liánkǎo 高中联考], and to universities [dàxué liánkǎo 大学联考], are also extremely competitive, with the National Taiwan University [Táiwān Dàxué 台湾大学] being the most sought after. Alternatives to the entrance examinations are under consideration in recent years.

Chinese students have many responsibilities at school. They are responsible for cleaning the classroom and maintaining discipline during class. Students take turns going to school early to clean their classrooms and the school grounds before the others arrive. There is no detention system but students are generally well-behaved. Assembly is held every morning and students exercise in the assembly grounds before going to class or during recess. In some schools in China, an eye exercise, accompanied by music, is practised during recess.

dì shíyī kè wǒ zhēn è
第十一课 我真饿

1 I am hungry

zhēn è
我真饿。
chī diǎnr dōngxi
我们去吃点儿东西吧！

xiǎng chī
你想吃什么？

xiǎng chī sānmíngzhì
我想吃三明治，
ne
你呢？

è kě
我不饿；我很渴。
xiǎng hē guǒzhī
我想喝果汁。

hànbǎobāo	bīngqílín	règǒu	niúnǎi
汉堡包	冰淇淋	热狗	牛奶

2 Do you like Chinese food?

你喜欢吃中国菜 (cài) 吗？

喜欢。
我妈妈会做 (zuò) 中国菜 (cài)。

真 (zhēn) 的啊 (a)！

我们全家 (quánjiā) 都 (dōu) 喜欢吃中国菜 (cài)。

我爸爸喜欢吃古老肉 (gǔlǎoròu)。

我妈妈喜欢吃柠檬鸡片 (níngméng-jīpiàn)。

我哥哥喜欢春卷 (chūnjuǎn)。

我妹妹喜欢炒饭 (chǎofàn)。

我最 (zuì) 喜欢炸虾片 (zháxiāpiàn)。

3 **Can you use chopsticks?**

ná kuàizi
你会不会拿筷子？

kěshì ná de kàn
我会，可是拿得不好。你看！

a ná de
啊！你拿得很好。

míngtiān dào
明天到我家吃饭吧！

tài le xièxie
太好了！谢谢你。

bié kèqi míngtiān jiàn
别客气，明天见。

明天见。

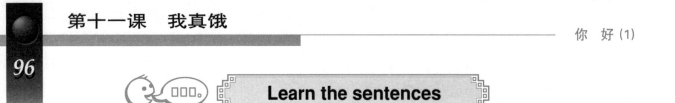

Learn the sentences

Expressing hunger or thirst

We learnt about stative verbs in lesson eight. The adjectives è 饿 and kě 渴 can also be used as stative verbs. Remember that when adjectives are used as stative verbs, you may add words such as hěn 很 (very), zhēn 真 (really) or, to make it negative, use bù 不 before the stative verb.

zhēn è 我 真 饿 。 kě 我 真 渴 。 他 很 饿 。	bú 我 不 饿 。 bù 我 不 渴 。 他 不 饿 。

Asking what someone would like to eat or drink

To ask What would you like to eat/drink? say Nǐ xiǎng chī/hē shénme? 你想吃 / 喝什么？ To answer the question, replace the question word shénme 什么 with the food/drink you would like to have.

xiǎng 你 想 吃 什 么 ？	hànbǎobāo 我 想 吃 汉 堡 包 。 bīngqílín 我 想 吃 冰 淇 淋 。
他 想 吃 什 么 ？	chǎofàn 他 想 吃 炒 饭 。 zháxiāpiàn 他 想 吃 炸 虾 片 。
hē 你 想 喝 什 么 ？	guǒzhī 我 想 喝 果 汁 。 niúnǎi 我 想 喝 牛 奶 。

Talking about someone's abilities

We learnt in lesson eight that to ask Can you speak Chinese? you say Nǐ huì bú huì shuō Hànyǔ? 你会不会说汉语？ Now the same sentence pattern will be used to ask about other things that people are able to do.

你会不会说汉语？ (Hànyǔ) 你会不会拿筷子？ (ná kuàizi) 你会不会做中国菜？ (zuò) 你会不会游泳？ (yóuyǒng) 你会不会踢足球？ (tī zúqiú)	{ 我会。 我不会。
他会不会说英语？ (Yīngyǔ) 他会不会骑车？ (qíchē) 他会不会打板球？ (bǎnqiú)	{ 他会。 他不会。

New words and expressions

饿	è	hungry
吃	chī	to eat
点儿	diǎnr	a little, a bit (short form of yìdiǎnr 一点儿)
东西	dōngxi	thing　dōng- east; xī- west
想	xiǎng	to feel like, to think
三明治	sānmíngzhì	sandwich
渴	kě	thirsty

喝	hē	to drink
果汁	guǒzhī	juice guǒ- fruit; zhī- juice
汉堡包	hànbǎobāo	hamburger (used in China), called hànbǎo 汉堡 in Taiwan
冰淇淋	bīngqílín	ice cream
热狗	règǒu	hotdog rè- hot; gǒu - dog
牛奶	niúnǎi	milk niú- cow; nǎi- milk
菜	cài	(meal) dish, vegetable
做	zuò	to make, to cook, to do
真的啊!	zhēn de a!	really!
全家	quánjiā	whole family quán- whole, all; jiā- family
古老肉	gǔlǎoròu	sweet and sour pork, a Cantonese dish, also called gūlūròu 咕噜肉 gǔ- ancient; lǎo- old; ròu- meat; gūlū- rumble
柠檬鸡片	níngméng-jīpiàn	lemon chicken níngméng- lemon; jī- chicken; piàn- thin piece
春卷	chūnjuǎn	spring rolls chūn- spring; juǎn- roll
炒饭	chǎofàn	fried rice chǎo- to stir-fry; fàn- cooked rice
炸虾片	zháxiāpiàn	prawn crackers zhá- to deep-fry; xiā- prawn; piàn- thin piece
拿	ná	to hold, to take
筷子	kuàizi	chopsticks
可是	kěshì	but
看	kàn	to look, to see
到	dào	to go to, to arrive
吃饭	chī fàn	to have a meal chī- to eat; fàn- meal, cooked rice
太好了	tài hǎo le	that's great! tài- too; hǎo- good; le- [stressing the situation]
别客气	bié kèqi	not at all, you're welcome bié- don't; kèqi- polite

Write the characters

真
zhēn
really

饿
è
hungry

吃
chī
to eat

想
xiǎng
to think

渴
kě
thirsty

喝
hē
to drink

菜
cài
dish, vegetable

饭
fàn
meal, cooked rice

Supplementary words

More food

汽水	qìshuǐ	soft drink, soda pop
水	shuǐ	water
开水	kāishuǐ	boiled water, drinking water
可乐	kělè	cola
面包	miànbāo	bread
炸薯条	zháshǔtiáo	French fries
黄油	huángyóu	butter, also called nǎiyóu 奶油
饼干	bǐnggān	biscuits
蛋糕	dàngāo	cake
面	miàn	noodles
汤	tāng	soup
乳酪	rǔlào	cheese
巧克力	qiǎokèlì	chocolate

Something to know

Chinese food

The three principles of Chinese food preparation are that the food should look good, smell good and taste good. Food is regarded as good if these three principles are satisfied. As China is vast, there is a great variety of foods and cooking methods. The Beijing style of cooking has lovely snacks, Sichuan cooking is well-known for its hot and spicy flavours, and Guangdong (Cantonese) cooking is famous for its sweet and sour style.

我会做中国菜.

盐　葱　生姜　大蒜　酱油

我会拿筷子.

我喜欢吃中国菜.

Seasonings and utensils

Despite the great variety in Chinese cooking, the most common seasonings are shallots, ginger, garlic and soy sauce.

Although many tools are used in cooking, the most unique Chinese cooking utensil is the wok [guōzi 锅子]. The wok serves many functions such as stir-frying, shallow-frying, deep-frying, steaming, and boiling.

On the table, apart from plates and soup bowls, chopsticks [kuàizi 筷子] and rice bowls [wǎn 碗] are essential items. Knives are considered unsuitable to be placed on the dinner table.

第十二课 复习

1 Letter to a friend

国明：

你好。我姓白，叫白大伟。我是澳大利亚人，会说一点儿汉语。我是学生，今年十二岁，上七年级。我家有五个人。我有爸爸、妈妈、一个哥哥和一个妹妹。我爸爸是医生，妈妈是护士，哥哥和妹妹都是学生。我家有一只狗。它很小、很可爱。

我们全家都喜欢吃中国菜。我妈妈会做中国菜。我最喜欢吃春卷。我有一个中国朋友，她叫李兰兰。兰兰和我同班，她说我筷子拿得很好。

我们的学校很大。我喜欢打板球，也喜欢游泳。你喜欢什么运动？

祝你

快乐

大伟

2 Being polite

Expressing thanks ⇨ **Responding**

xièxie
谢 谢 。

kèqi
不 客 气 。

xièxie
谢 谢 你 。

bié kèqi
别 客 气 。

Expressing welcome ⇨ **Responding**

huānyíng
欢 迎 , 欢 迎 。

xièxie
谢 谢 。

qǐng jìn
请 进 。

Apologising ⇨ **Responding**

duìbuqǐ
对 不 起 。

guānxi
没 关 系 。

Praising people ⇨ **Responding**

de
你 说 得 很 好 。

nǎli
哪 里 !

ná
你 拿 得 很 好 。

哪 里 ! 哪 里 !

zuò
你 做 得 很 好 。

Asking for help

qǐngwèn
请 问 , … … ?

3 Reading signs

Appendix

WORDS AND EXPRESSIONS
Chinese-English

Simplified	Pinyin	English	Traditional	Lesson
A 啊	a	[an exclamation]	啊	4
爱尔兰	Ài'ěrlán	Ireland	愛爾蘭	8
澳大利亚	Àodàlìyà	Australia	澳大利亞	8
澳洲	Àozhōu	Australia (used in Taiwan)	澳洲	8
B 八	bā	eight	八	3
把手放下	bǎ shǒu fàng xià	put down (your) hand	把手放下	2
把书打开	bǎ shū dǎ kāi	open (your) book	把書打開	2
爸爸	bàba	dad, father	爸爸	6
吧	ba	[indicating suggestion]	吧	9
白	Bái	a family name; bái- white	白	2
百	bǎi	hundred	百	3
板球	bǎnqiú	cricket	板球	9
棒球	bàngqiú	baseball	棒球	9
保龄球	bǎolíngqiú	bowling (tenpin)	保齡球	9
保罗	Bǎoluó	Paul	保羅	6
鼻子	bízi	nose	鼻子	10
笔	bǐ	pen	筆	5
蝙蝠	biānfú	bat	蝙蝠	7
别客气	bié kèqi	you're welcome, not at all	別客氣	11
冰淇淋	bīngqílín	ice cream	冰淇淋	11
饼干	bǐnggān	biscuits	餅乾	11
伯伯	bóbo	father's elder brother	伯伯	6
不会	bú huì	unable to, cannot	不會	8
不客气	bú kèqi	you're welcome, not at all	不客氣	5
不去	bú qù	not going	不去	9
不是	bú shì	no (negative form of shì 是)	不是	5
不要说话	bú yào shuōhuà	do not talk	不要說話	2
不	bù	no, not (used to negate)	不	5
C 彩笔	cǎibǐ	colour pencil	彩筆	5
菜	cài	meal, dish, vegetable	菜	11
苍蝇	cāngying	fly (n.)	蒼蠅	7
长	cháng	long	長	10
炒饭	chǎofàn	fried rice	炒飯	11
乘以	chéng yǐ	multiplied by	乘以	3
吃	chī	to eat	吃	11

Simplified	Pinyin	English	Traditional	Lesson
吃饭	chī fàn	to have a meal	吃飯	11
尺	chǐ	ruler	尺	5
宠物	chǒngwù	pet	寵物	7
除以	chú yǐ	divided by	除以	3
窗户	chuānghu	window	窗戶	5
春卷	chūnjuǎn	spring rolls	春捲	11

	Simplified	Pinyin	English	Traditional	Lesson
D	打	dǎ	to hit, to play (basket ball, tennis...etc.)	打	9
	大	dà	big, large	大	7
	大概	dàgài	probably	大概	5
	大声点儿	dà shēng diǎnr	a little louder	大聲點兒	2
	大伟	Dàwěi	David	大偉	2
	大熊猫	dàxióngmāo	giant panda	大熊貓	7
	袋鼠	dàishǔ	kangaroo	袋鼠	7
	蛋糕	dàngāo	cake	蛋糕	11
	到	dào	to go to, to arrive	到	11
	到前面来	dào qiánmian lái	come to the front	到前面來	2
	德国	Déguó	Germany	德國	8
	德语	Déyǔ	German language	德語	8
	的	de	[possessive particle]	的	5
	得	de	[used after a verb to indicate degree or result]	得	8
	等于	děng yú	be equal to	等於	3
	弟弟	dìdi	younger brother	弟弟	6
	第二	dì èr	second	第二	3
	第二课	dì èr kè	lesson two	第二課	3
	第三	dì sān	third	第三	3
	第三课	dì sān kè	lesson three	第三課	3
	第一	dì yī	first	第一	3
	第一课	dì yī kè	lesson one	第一課	3
	点儿	diǎnr	a little, a bit (short form of yìdiǎnr 一点儿)	點兒	11
	东西	dōngxi	thing	東西	11
	动物	dòngwù	animal	動物	7
	都	dōu	all	都	7
	短	duǎn	short	短	10
	对不起	duìbuqǐ	excuse me, sorry	對不起	8

	Simplified	Pinyin	English	Traditional	Lesson
E	俄罗斯	Éluósī	Russia	俄羅斯	8
	饿	è	hungry	餓	11
	鳄鱼	èyú	crocodile	鱷魚	7
	儿子	érzi	son	兒子	6
	耳朵	ěrduo	ear	耳朵	10
	二	èr	two	二	3

	Simplified	Pinyin	English	Traditional	Lesson
F	法国	Fǎguó	France	法國	8
	非常好	fēicháng hǎo	extremely good	非常好	2
	菲律宾	Fēilùbīn	the Philippines	菲律賓	8
	粉笔	fěnbǐ	chalk	粉筆	5

	Simplified	Pinyin	English	Traditional	Lesson
G	橄榄球	gǎnlǎnqiú	rugby, football	橄欖球	9
	高尔夫球	gāo'ěrfūqiú	golf	高爾夫球	9
	哥哥	gēge	elder brother	哥哥	6
	个	gè	[measure word]	個	6
	工人	gōngrén	labourer, worker	工人	6
	狗	gǒu	dog	狗	7
	姑姑	gūgu	father's sister	姑姑	6
	咕噜肉	gūlūròu	sweet and sour pork, a Cantonese dish	咕嚕肉	11
	古老肉	gǔlǎoròu	sweet and sour pork, a Cantonese dish	咕咾肉	11
	国	guó	country	國	8
	果汁	guǒzhī	juice	果汁	11
H	汉堡	hànbǎo	hamburger (used in Taiwan)	漢堡	11
	汉堡包	hànbǎobāo	hamburger (used in China)	漢堡包	11
	汉语	Hànyǔ	Chinese language	漢語	8
	好	hǎo	good, well	好	2
	好啊	hǎo a	good! (agreeing)	好啊	9
	好吗	hǎo ma	OK? (asking for agreement)	好嗎	9
	喝	hē	to drink	喝	11
	和	hé	and	和	5
	黑板	hēibǎn	blackboard	黑板	5
	黑板擦	hēibǎncā	blackboard duster	黑板擦	5
	很	hěn	very	很	7
	很好	hěn hǎo	very good	很好	2
	猴子	hóuzi	monkey	猴子	7
	蝴蝶	húdié	butterfly	蝴蝶	7
	护士	hùshi	nurse	護士	6
	欢迎	huānyíng	welcome	歡迎	4
	黄油	huángyóu	butter, also called nǎiyóu 奶油	黃油	11
	会	huì	can, to be able to	會	8
J	鸡	jī	chicken, rooster	雞	7
	几	jǐ	how many	幾	4
	继父	jìfù	stepfather	繼父	6
	继母	jìmǔ	stepmother	繼母	6
	家	jiā	family, home	家	6
	加	jiā	plus, to add	加	3
	加拿大	Jiānádà	Canada	加拿大	8
	减	jiǎn	minus, to subtract	減	3
	剪刀	jiǎndāo	scissors	剪刀	5
	见	jiàn	to see	見	2
	胶水	jiāoshuǐ	glue	膠水	5
	叫	jiào	to be called, to call	叫	6
	教室	jiàoshì	classroom	教室	5
	姐姐	jiějie	elder sister	姊姊，姐姐	6
	今年	jīnnián	this year	今年	4

Simplified	Pinyin	English	Traditional	Lesson
金鱼	jīnyú	goldfish	金魚	7
九	jiǔ	nine	九	3
舅舅	jiùjiu	mother's brother	舅舅	6
K 开水	kāishuǐ	drinking water, boiled water	開水	11
看	kàn	to look, to see	看	11
看黑板	kàn hēibǎn	look at the blackboard	看黑板	2
渴	kě	thirsty	渴	11
可爱	kě'ài	lovely	可愛	7
可乐	kělè	cola	可樂	11
可是	kěshì	but	可是	11
口	kǒu	mouth	口	1
快乐	kuàilè	happy	快樂	4
筷子	kuàizi	chopsticks	筷子	11
L 兰兰	Lánlan	a given name	蘭蘭	2
篮球	lánqiú	basketball	籃球	9
老虎	lǎohǔ	tiger	老虎	7
老师	lǎoshī	teacher	老師	2
老鼠	lǎoshǔ	mouse, rat	老鼠	7
垒球	lěiqiú	softball	壘球	9
李	Lǐ	a family name; lǐ- plum	李	2
丽丽	Lìli	Lily	麗麗	6
脸	liǎn	face	臉	10
两	liǎng	two	兩	4
林	Lín	a family name; lín-forest	林	2
○	líng	zero	○	3
六	liù	six	六	3
龙	lóng	dragon	龍	7
M 妈妈	māma	mum, mother	媽媽	6
马	mǎ	horse	馬	7
马克	Mǎkè	Mark	馬克	4
马来西亚	Mǎláixīyà	Malaysia	馬來西亞	8
蚂蚁	mǎyǐ	ant	螞蟻	7
吗	ma	[question word]	嗎	5
忙	máng	busy	忙	9
猫	māo	cat	貓	7
毛笔	máobǐ	writing brush	毛筆	5
没	méi	[negative word]	沒	6
没关系	méi guānxi	it doesn't matter, that's all right	沒關係	8
没有	méi yǒu	not have	沒有	6
眉毛	méimao	eyebrow	眉毛	10
美国	Měiguó	America, USA	美國	8
美怡	Měiyí	a given name	美怡	10
妹妹	mèimei	younger sister	妹妹	6
门	mén	door	門	5

Simplified	Pinyin	English	Traditional	Lesson
们	men	[plural word]	們	2
蜜蜂	mìfēng	bee	蜜蜂	7
面	miàn	noodles	麵	11
面包	miànbāo	bread	麵包	11
明天	míngtiān	tomorrow	明天	2
名字	míngzi	name	名字	6
墨西哥	Mòxīgē	Mexico	墨西哥	8
N 拿	ná	to take, to hold	拿	11
哪	nǎ	which	哪	8
哪里	nǎli	not at all (said when praised; literally where)	哪裡	8
那	nà	that	那	5
奶奶	nǎinai	grandma, grandmother	奶奶	6
奶油	nǎiyóu	butter, also called huángyóu 黄油	奶油	11
南非	Nánfēi	South Africa	南非	8
呢	ne	[question word]	呢	6
你	nǐ	you (singular)	你	2
你的	nǐ de	your, yours	你的	5
你好	nǐ hǎo	hello, how do you do	你好	2
你们	nǐmen	you (plural)	你們	2
年级	niánjí	grade	年級	10
鸟	niǎo	bird	鳥	7
柠檬鸡片	níngméng-jīpiàn	lemon chicken	檸檬雞片	11
牛	niú	cow, ox	牛	7
牛奶	niúnǎi	milk	牛奶	11
纽西兰	Niǔxīlán	New Zealand (used in Taiwan)	紐西蘭	8
女儿	nǚ'ér	daughter	女兒	6
P 排球	páiqiú	volleyball	排球	9
跑步	pǎobù	running, to jog	跑步	9
跑来跑去	pǎolái-pǎoqù	to run around	跑來跑去	7
朋友	péngyou	friend	朋友	10
匹	pǐ	[measure word for horses]	匹	7
乒乓球	pīngpāngqiú	table tennis	乒乓球	9
Q 七	qī	seven	七	3
妻子	qīzi	wife	妻子	6
骑车	qíchē	cycling, to ride a bicycle	騎車	9
汽水	qìshuǐ	soft drink, soda pop	汽水	11
铅笔	qiānbǐ	pencil	鉛筆	5
铅笔盒	qiānbǐhé	pencil case	鉛筆盒	5
巧克力	qiǎokèlì	chocolate	巧克力	11
请安静	qǐng ānjìng	quiet please	請安靜	2
请回座位	qǐng huí zuòwèi	return to (your) seat please	請回座位	2
请进	qǐng jìn	come in please	請進	2
请举手	qǐng jǔshǒu	please raise (your) hand	請舉手	2
请坐	qǐng zuò	sit down please	請坐	2

Simplified	Pinyin	English	Traditional	Lesson
请坐好	qǐng zuò hǎo	sit properly please	請坐好	2
请问	qǐngwèn	may I ask	請問	8
曲棍球	qūgùnqiú	hockey	曲棍球	9
去	qù	to go	去	9
全家	quánjiā	whole family	全家	11
R 热狗	règǒu	hotdog	熱狗	11
人	rén	person, people	人	1
日本	Rìběn	Japan	日本	8
日语	Rìyǔ	Japanese language	日語	8
乳酪	rǔlào	cheese	乳酪	11
瑞士	Ruìshì	Switzerland	瑞士	8
S 三	sān	three	三	3
三明治	sānmíngzhì	sandwich	三明治	11
山	shān	mountain	山	1
上	shàng	to go, to attend; up	上	10
蛇	shé	snake, serpent	蛇	7
谁	shéi	who, whom	誰	4
谁的	shéi de	whose	誰的	5
什么	shénme	what	什麼	5
生日	shēngrì	birthday	生日	4
十	shí	ten	十	3
是	shì	am, is, are	是	2
是啊	shì a	yes, yeah (shows agreement)	是啊	7
是的	shìde	yes (alternative of shì 是 in answering question)	是的	5
书	shū	book	書	5
书包	shūbāo	school bag	書包	5
叔叔	shūshu	father's younger brother	叔叔	6
树熊	shùxióng	koala (used in China)	樹熊	3
水	shuǐ	water	水	11
说	shuō	to speak, to say	說	8
说话	shuōhuà	to talk, to speak, to say	說話	10
四	sì	four	四	3
岁	suì	year of age	歲	4
T 他	tā	he, him	他	2
她	tā	she, her	她	4
它	tā	it	牠, 它	7
它们	tāmen	they (plural of it)	牠們, 它們	7
台湾	Táiwān	Taiwan	臺灣	8
太好了	tài hǎo le	that's great!	太好了	11
太太	tàitai	Mrs, wife	太太	6
泰国	Tàiguó	Thailand	泰國	8
汤	tāng	soup	湯	11
踢	tī	to kick, to play (soccer)	踢	9
体操	tǐcāo	gymnastics	體操	9

Simplified	Pinyin	English	Traditional	Lesson
田径	tiánjìng	track and field	田徑	9
条	tiáo	[measure word for long, thin objects]	條	7
跳高	tiàogāo	high jump	跳高	9
跳远	tiàoyuǎn	long jump	跳遠	9
同班	tóngbān	same class	同班	10
同学	tóngxué	fellow student, schoolmate	同學	2
同学们	tóngxuémen	fellow students (plural)	同學們	2
头	tóu	head	頭	10
头发	tóufa	hair (on human head)	頭髮	10
兔子	tùzi	rabbit, hare	兔子	7

Simplified	Pinyin	English	Traditional	Lesson
W 王	Wáng	a family name; wáng- king	王	10
网球	wǎngqiú	tennis	網球	9
喂	wèi	hey!	喂	9
蚊子	wénzi	mosquito	蚊子	7
我	wǒ	I, me	我	2
我的	wǒ de	my, mine	我的	5
我们走吧	wǒmen zǒu ba	let's go	我們走吧	9
无尾熊	wúwěixióng	koala (used in Taiwan)	無尾熊	7
五	wǔ	five	五	3

Simplified	Pinyin	English	Traditional	Lesson
X 西班牙	Xībānyá	Spain	西班牙	8
希腊	Xīlà	Greece	希臘	8
喜欢	xǐhuān	to like	喜歡	9
先生	xiānsheng	Mr, husband	先生	6
香港	Xiānggǎng	Hong Kong	香港	8
想	xiǎng	to feel like, to think	想	11
橡皮	xiàngpí	eraser	橡皮	5
小	xiǎo	small, little (in size)	小	7
小妹妹	xiǎomèimei	little girl	小妹妹	8
小明	Xiǎomíng	a given name	小明	5
笑哈哈	xiàohāha	to laugh heartily, laughingly	笑哈哈	10
谢谢	xièxie	thanks	謝謝	4
新加坡	Xīnjiāpō	Singapore	新加坡	8
新几内亚	Xīnjǐnèiyà	New Guinea	新幾內亞	8
新西兰	Xīnxīlán	New Zealand (used in China)	新西蘭	8
姓	xìng	family name, surname	姓	6
凶	xiōng	fierce, ferocious	凶	7
凶巴巴	xiōngbāba	fiercely, ferociously	凶巴巴	10
熊猫	xióngmāo	panda	熊貓	7
学生	xuésheng	student, pupil	學生	6
学校	xuéxiào	school	學校	10

Simplified	Pinyin	English	Traditional	Lesson
Y 鸭子	yāzi	duck	鴨子	7
眼睛	yǎnjing	eye	眼睛	10
羊	yáng	goat, ram	羊	7
爷爷	yéye	grandad, grandfather	爺爺	6

Simplified	Pinyin	English	Traditional	Lesson
也	yě	also, too	也	6
一	yī	one	一	3
一点儿	yìdiǎnr	a little, a bit	一點兒	8
医生	yīshēng	doctor	醫生	6
姨	yí	mother's sister	姨	6
咦	yí	why!, huh! (indicating surprise)	咦	8
椅子	yǐzi	chair	椅子	5
意大利	Yìdàlì	Italy	義大利	8
印度	Yìndù	India	印度	8
英国	Yīngguó	England	英國	8
英语	Yīngyǔ	English language	英語	8
游泳	yóuyǒng	swimming, to swim	游泳	9
有	yǒu	to have, there is/are	有	6
鱼	yú	fish	魚	7
圆珠笔	yuánzhūbǐ	biro, ballpoint pen (used in China)	圓珠筆	5
原子笔	yuánzǐbǐ	biro, ballpoint pen (used in Taiwan)	原子筆	5
越南	Yuènán	Vietnam	越南	8
运动	yùndòng	sports, exercise	運動	9
Z 再见	zàijiàn	goodbye	再見	2
再说一次	zài shuō yí cì	say (it) again	再說一次	2
早	zǎo	morning, early	早	2
炸薯条	zháshǔtiáo	French fries	炸薯條	11
炸虾片	zháxiāpiàn	prawn crackers	炸蝦片	11
站起来	zhàn qǐlai	stand up	站起來	2
蟑螂	zhāngláng	cockroach	蟑螂	7
丈夫	zhàngfu	husband	丈夫	6
这	zhè	this	這	5
真	zhēn	really	真	7
真的啊	zhēnde a	really!	真的啊	11
只	zhī	[measure word for dogs, cats, birds]	隻	7
知道	zhīdao	to know	知道	5
纸	zhǐ	paper	紙	5
中国	Zhōngguó	China	中國	8
猪	zhū	pig, boar	豬	7
祝	zhù	to wish (offer good wishes)	祝	4
注意听	zhùyì tīng	listen carefully	注意聽	2
桌子	zhuōzi	desk	桌子	5
走	zǒu	to go, to walk	走	9
走吧	zǒu ba	let's go!	走吧	9
足球	zúqiú	soccer	足球	9
嘴巴	zuǐba	mouth	嘴巴	10
最	zuì	most	最	9
做	zuò	to make, to cook, to do	做	11

WORDS AND EXPRESSIONS
English-Chinese

English	Pinyin	Simplified
Grammar:		
degree or result	de	得
exclamation	a	啊
negative word	bù	不
	méi	没
possessive particle	de	的
question word	ma	吗
	ne	呢
suggestion	ba	吧
Plural form:		
	men	们
Measure words:		
dogs, cats, birds	zhī	只
fish	tiáo	条
horses	pǐ	匹
people	gè	个
Family names:		
	Bái	白
	Lǐ	李
	Lín	林
	Mǎ	马
	Shānkǒu	山口 (Japanese)
	Wáng	王
Given names:		
	Dàlì	大利
	Dàmíng	大明
	Dàzhōng	大中
	Guómíng	国明
	Jiǔshān	九山
	Lánlan	兰兰
	Měiyí	美怡
	Sānshān	三山
	Xiǎoguó	小国
	Xiǎomáo	小毛
	Xiǎoměi	小美
	Xiǎomíng	小明
David	Dàwěi	大伟
Lily	Lìli	丽丽
Mark	Mǎkè	马克
A		
a little, a bit	diǎnr, yìdiǎnr	点儿, 一点儿
a little louder	dà shēng diǎnr	大声点儿
able to, can	huì	会
age: year of-	suì	岁

English	Pinyin	Simplified
all	dōu	都
also, too	yě	也
am, is, are	shì	是
am not	bú shì	不是
America, USA	Měiguó	美国
and	hé	和
animal	dòngwù	动物
ant	mǎyǐ	蚂蚁
are, is, am	shì	是
are not	bú shì	不是
arrive, to go to	dào	到
attend (school, work)	shàng	上
aunt (father's sister)	gūgu	姑姑
(mother's sister)	yí	姨
Australia	Àodàlìyà	澳大利亚
(in Taiwan)	Àozhōu	澳洲
B		
badminton	yǔmáoqiú	羽毛球
ballpoint pen	yuánzhūbǐ	圆珠笔
baseball	bàngqiú	棒球
basketball	lánqiú	篮球
bat	biānfú	蝙蝠
bee	mìfēng	蜜蜂
big, large	dà	大
bird	niǎo	鸟
biro	yuánzhūbǐ	圆珠笔
birthday	shēngrì	生日
biscuits	bǐnggān	饼干
blackboard	hēibǎn	黑板
blackboard duster	hēibǎncā	黑板擦
boar, pig	zhū	猪
boiled water	kāishuǐ	开水
book	shū	书
bowling: tenpin-	bǎolíngqiú	保龄球
bread	miànbāo	面包
brother: elder-	gēge	哥哥
brother: younger-	dìdi	弟弟
brush : writing-	máobǐ	毛笔
busy	máng	忙
but	kěshì	可是
butter	huángyóu, nǎiyóu	黄油, 奶油
butterfly	húdié	蝴蝶
C		
cake	dàngāo	蛋糕

English	Pinyin	Simplified	English	Pinyin	Simplified
call (*v.*), to be called	jiào	叫	duck	yāzi	鸭子
can, to be able to	huì	会	**E**		
Canada	Jiānádà	加拿大	ear	ěrduo	耳朵
Canadian	Jiānádàrén	加拿大人	early, morning	zǎo	早
cannot, unable to	bú huì	不会	eat	chī	吃
cat	māo	猫	eight	bā	八
chair	yǐzi	椅子	elder brother	gēge	哥哥
chalk	fěnbǐ	粉笔	elder sister	jiějie	姐姐
cheese	rǔlào	乳酪	England	Yīngguó	英国
chicken, rooster	jī	鸡	English language	Yīngyǔ	英语
China	Zhōngguó	中国	Englishman	Yīngguórén	英国人
Chinese language	Hànyǔ	汉语	equal to	děngyú	等于
(in China)	Pǔtōnghuà	普通话	eraser	xiàngpí	橡皮
(in Taiwan)	Guóyǔ	国语	excuse me, sorry	duìbuqǐ	对不起
Chinese (person)	Zhōngguórén	中国人	exercise, sports	yùndòng	运动
chocolate	qiǎokèlì	巧克力	extremely good	fēicháng hǎo	非常好
chopsticks	kuàizi	筷子	eye	yǎnjing	眼睛
Christian name	míngzi	名字	eyebrow	méimao	眉毛
classroom	jiàoshì	教室	**F**		
cockroach	zhāngláng	蟑螂	face	liǎn	脸
cola	kělè	可乐	family, home	jiā	家
colour pencil	cǎibǐ	彩笔	family name	xìng	姓
come in please	qǐng jìn	请进	father, dad	bàba	爸爸
come to the front	dào qiánmian lái	到前面来	father's elder brother	bóbo	伯伯
cook (*v.*), to make	zuò	做	father's sister	gūgu	姑姑
cookies	bǐnggān	饼干	father's younger brother	shūshu	叔叔
country	guó	国	feel like, to think	xiǎng	想
cow, ox	niú	牛	fellow student	tóngxué	同学
cricket	bǎnqiú	板球	fellow students	tóngxuémen	同学们
crocodile	èyú	鳄鱼	ferocious, fierce	xiōng,	凶,
cycling, ride a bicycle	qíchē	骑车	ferociously, fiercely	xiōngbāba	凶巴巴
D			first	dì yī	第一
dad, father	bàba	爸爸	first name	míngzi	名字
daughter	nǚ'ér	女儿	fish	yú	鱼
David	Dàwěi	大伟	five	wǔ	五
desk	zhuōzi	桌子	fly (*n.*)	cāngying	苍蝇
dish, meal, vegetable	cài	菜	football (soccer)	zúqiú	足球
divided by	chú yǐ	除以	football (rugby)	gǎnlǎnqiú	橄榄球
do, to make, to cook	zuò	做	four	sì	四
do not talk	bú yào shuōhuà	不要说话	France	Fǎguó	法国
doctor	yīshēng	医生	French fries	zháshǔtiáo	炸薯条
dog	gǒu	狗	fried rice	chǎofàn	炒饭
don't mention it,	bú kèqi,	不客气,	friend	péngyou	朋友
you are welcome	bié kèqi	别客气	**G**		
door	mén	门	German language	Déyǔ	德语
dragon	lóng	龙	German (person)	Déguórén	德国人
drink (*v.*)	hē	喝	Germany	Déguó	德国
drinking water	kāishuǐ	开水	glue	jiāoshuǐ	胶水

English	Pinyin	Simplified	English	Pinyin	Simplified
go	qù	去	ice cream	bīngqílín	冰淇淋
go, to attend; up	shàng	上	India	Yìndù	印度
go, to walk	zǒu	走	Ireland	Ài'ěrlán	爱尔兰
go to, to arrive	dào	到	is, are, am	shì	是
goat, ram	yáng	羊	is not	búshì	不是
goldfish	jīnyú	金鱼	it	tā	它
golf	gāo'ěrfūqiú	高尔夫球	it doesn't matter	méi guānxi	没关系
good! (agreeing)	hǎo a	好啊	Italy	Yìdàlì	意大利
good, well	hǎo	好	its	tāde	它的
goodbye	zàijiàn	再见	**J**		
grade (school)	niánjí	年级	Japan	Rìběn	日本
grandad	yéye	爷爷	Japanese language	Rìyǔ	日语
grandma	nǎinai	奶奶	Japanese (person)	Rìběnrén	日本人
Greece	Xīlà	希腊	jogging, running	pǎobù	跑步
gymnastics	tǐcāo	体操	juice	guǒzhī	果汁
H			**K**		
hair (on human head)	tóufa	头发	kangaroo	dàishǔ	袋鼠
hamburger (in China)	hànbǎobāo	汉堡包	kick	tī	踢
(in Taiwan)	hànbǎo	汉堡	know	zhīdao	知道
happy	kuàilè	快乐	koala (in China)	kǎolā, shùxióng	考拉,树熊
have/has	yǒu	有	(in Taiwan)	wúwěixióng	无尾熊
have a meal	chīfàn	吃饭	**L**		
he, him	tā	他	labourer	gōngrén	工人
head	tóu	头	large, big	dà	大
hello, how do you do	nǐ hǎo	你好	laughingly	xiàohāha	笑哈哈
her	tāde	她的	lemon chicken	níngméng-jīpiàn	柠檬鸡片
her, she	tā	她	lesson one	dì yī kè	第一课
hers	tā de	她的	lesson three	dì sān kè	第三课
hey!	wèi	喂	lesson two	dì èr kè	第二课
high jump	tiàogāo	跳高	let's go	wǒmen zǒu ba	我们走吧
him, he	tā	他	like (v.)	xǐhuān	喜欢
his	tā de	他的	listen carefully	zhùyì tīng	注意听
hit	dǎ	打	little (in size), small	xiǎo	小
hockey	qūgùnqiú	曲棍球	little: a-, a bit	yìdiǎnr	一点儿
hold, to take	ná	拿	little girl	xiǎomèimei	小妹妹
home, family	jiā	家	long	cháng	长
Hong Kong	Xiānggǎng	香港	long jump	tiàoyuǎn	跳远
horse	mǎ	马	look, to see	kàn	看
hotdog	règǒu	热狗	look at the blackboard	kàn hēibǎn	看黑板
how do you do, hello	nǐ hǎo	你好	louder	dà shēng diǎnr	大声点儿
how many	jǐ	几	lovely	kě'ài	可爱
huh! (surprise)	yí	咦	**M**		
hundred	bǎi	百	make, to cook, to do	zuò	做
hungry	è	饿	Malaysia	Mǎláixīyà	马来西亚
husband	zhàngfu	丈夫	Mark	Mǎkè	马克
husband, Mr	xiānsheng	先生	may I ask	qǐngwèn	请问
I			me, I	wǒ	我
I, me	wǒ	我	meal, dish, vegetable	cài	菜

English	Pinyin	Simplified	English	Pinyin	Simplified
meal: to have a-	chī fàn	吃饭	people, person	rén	人
Mexico	Mòxīgē	墨西哥	pet	chǒngwù	宠物
milk (cow's)	niúnǎi	牛奶	Philippines	Fēilǜbīn	菲律宾
mine, my	wǒ de	我的	pig, boar	zhū	猪
minus	jiǎn	减	play (basketball, tennis)	dǎ	打
monkey	hóuzi	猴子	(soccer)	tī	踢
morning, early	zǎo	早	plus	jiā	加
mosquito	wénzi	蚊子	prawn crackers	zháxiāpiàn	炸虾片
most	zuì	最	probably	dàgài	大概
mother, mum	māma	妈妈	pupil, student	xuésheng	学生
mother's sister	yí	姨	put down (your) hand	bǎ shǒu fàng xià	把手放下
(in Taiwan)	āyí	阿姨	**Q**		
mother's brother	jiùjiu	舅舅	quiet please	qǐng ānjìng	请安静
mountain	shān	山	**R**		
mouse, rat	lǎoshǔ	老鼠	rabbit, hare	tùzi	兔子
mouth	kǒu,	口,	raise (your) hand plse.	qǐng jǔshǒu	请举手
	zuǐba	嘴巴	rat, mouse	lǎoshǔ	老鼠
Mr, husband	xiānsheng	先生	really	zhēn	真
Mrs, wife	tàitai	太太	really!	zhēnde a!	真的啊！
multiplied by	chéng yǐ	乘以	return to (your) seat plse.	qǐng huí zuòwèi	请回座位
my, mine	wǒ de	我的	ride a bicycle	qíchē	骑车
N			rugby, football	gǎnlǎnqiú	橄榄球
name	míngzi	名字	ruler (measure)	chǐ	尺
New Guinea	Xīnjǐnèiyà	新几内亚	run around	pǎolái-pǎoqù	跑来跑去
New Zealand (in China)	Xīnxīlán	新西兰	running, to jog	pǎobù	跑步
(in Taiwan)	Niǔxīlán	纽西兰	Russia	Éluósī	俄罗斯
New Zealander	Xīnxīlánrén	新西兰人	**S**		
nine	jiǔ	九	same class	tóngbān	同班
no	bú shì	不是	sandwich	sānmíngzhì	三明治
noodles	miàn	面	say, talk	shuōhuà	说话
nose	bízi	鼻子	say (it) again	zài shuō yí cì	再说一次
not (to form negative)	bù	不	school	xuéxiào	学校
not at all (when praised)	nǎli	哪里	school bag	shūbāo	书包
(when thanked)	bú kèqi	不客气	schoolmate	tóngxué	同学
not going	bú qù	不去	schoolmates	tóngxuémen	同学们
not have	méi yǒu	没有	scissors	jiǎndāo	剪刀
nurse	hùshi	护士	second	dì èr	第二
O			see, catch sight of	jiàn	见
OK?	hǎo ma	好吗	see, look	kàn	看
one	yī	一	seven	qī	七
open (your) book	bǎ shū dǎkāi	把书打开	she, her	tā	她
P			short	duǎn	短
panda	xióngmāo	熊猫	Singapore	Xīnjiāpō	新加坡
paper	zhǐ	纸	sister (elder)	jiějie	姐姐
Paul	Bǎoluó	保罗	(younger)	mèimei	妹妹
pen	bǐ	笔	sit down please	qǐng zuò	请坐
pencil	qiānbǐ	铅笔	sit properly please	qǐng zuò hǎo	请坐好
pencil case	qiānbǐhé	铅笔盒	six	liù	六

English	Pinyin	Simplified
small	xiǎo	小
snake, serpent	shé	蛇
soccer	zúqiú	足球
soft drink, soda pop	qìshuǐ	汽水
softball	lěiqiú	垒球
son	érzi	儿子
sorry, excuse me	duìbuqǐ	对不起
soup	tāng	汤
South Africa	Nánfēi	南非
Spain	Xībānyá	西班牙
speak	shuō,	说,
	shuōhuà	说话
sports, exercise	yùndòng	运动
spring rolls	chūnjuǎn	春卷
stand up	zhàn qǐlai	站起来
stepfather	jìfù	继父
stepmother	jìmǔ	继母
student	xuésheng	学生
surname	xìng	姓
sweet and sour pork	gǔlǎoròu,	古老肉,
	gūlūròu	咕噜肉
swimming, to swim	yóuyǒng	游泳
Switzerland	Ruìshì	瑞士

T

English	Pinyin	Simplified
table tennis	pīngpāngqiú	乒乓球
Taiwan	Táiwān	台湾
take, to hold	ná	拿
talk	shuōhuà	说话
teacher	lǎoshī	老师
ten	shí	十
tennis	wǎngqiú	网球
Thailand	Tàiguó	泰国
thank you	xièxie nǐ	谢谢你
thanks	xièxie	谢谢
that	nà	那
that's all right, it doesn't matter	méi guānxi	没关系
that's great!	tài hǎo le	太好了
there is/are	yǒu	有
they (people)	tāmen	他们
(animal, object)	tāmen	它们
thing	dōngxi	东西
think, feel like	xiǎng	想
third	dì sān	第三
thirsty	kě	渴
this	zhè	这
this year	jīnnián	今年
three	sān	三

English	Pinyin	Simplified
tiger	lǎohǔ	老虎
tomorrow	míngtiān	明天
too, also	yě	也
track and field	tiánjìng	田径
two	èr, liǎng	二, 两

U

unable to, cannot	bú huì	不会
uncle (mother's brother)	jiùjiu	舅舅
(father's elder brother)	bóbo	伯伯
(father's younger brother)	shūshu	叔叔
USA, America	Měiguó	美国

V

vegetable, dish, meal	cài	菜
very	hěn	很
very good	hěn hǎo	很好
Vietnam	Yuènán	越南
volleyball	páiqiú	排球

W

English	Pinyin	Simplified
water	shuǐ	水
welcome	huānyíng	欢迎
well, good	hǎo	好
what	shénme	什么
which	nǎ	哪
white	bái	白
who, whom	shéi	谁
whole family	quánjiā	全家
whose	shéi de	谁的
why!, huh! (indicating surprise)	yí	咦
wife	qīzi	妻子
wife, Mrs	tàitai	太太
window	chuānghu	窗户
wish (offer good wishes)	zhù	祝
worker, labourer	gōngrén	工人
writing brush	máobǐ	毛笔

Y

English	Pinyin	Simplified
year of age	suì	岁
yes	shìde	是的
yes!	shì a	是啊
you (singular)	nǐ	你
(plural)	nǐmen	你们
(polite)	nín	您
you're welcome	bié kèqi,	别客气,
	bú kèqi	不客气
younger brother	dìdi	弟弟
younger sister	mèimei	妹妹
your, yours	nǐ de	你的

Z

English	Pinyin	Simplified
zero	líng	〇

LEARN TO WRITE
by lesson

	Chinese		English		Chinese		English
1	人	rén	people, person	**7**	宠	chǒng	to spoil
	山	shān	mountain		物	wù	object, thing
	口	kǒu	mouth		只	zhī	(measure word)
					狗	gǒu	dog
2	你	nǐ	you		马	mǎ	horse
	好	hǎo	good		很	hěn	very
	我	wǒ	I, me		大	dà	big
	是	shì	is, am, are		小	xiǎo	little
	他	tā	he, him		没	méi	(negative word)
	们	men	(plural word)				
				8	中	zhōng	centre, middle
3	一	yī	one		国	guó	nation
	二	èr	two		澳	ào	bay
	三	sān	three		利	lì	sharp
	四	sì	four		亚	yà	second
	五	wǔ	five		也	yě	also
	六	liù	six		会	huì	to be able to, can
	七	qī	seven		说	shuō	to speak, to say
	八	bā	eight				
	九	jiǔ	nine	**9**	喜	xǐ	to like; happy
	十	shí	ten		欢	huān	happy
					运	yùn	to transport; luck
4	谁	shéi	who		动	dòng	to move
	她	tā	she, her		打	dǎ	to hit, to play (tennis...etc.)
	老	lǎo	old		球	qiú	ball
	师	shī	teacher		去	qù	to go
	几	jǐ	how many		吧	ba	(suggestion word)
	岁	suì	year of age				
	两	liǎng	two	**10**	朋	péng	friend
					友	yǒu	friend
5	这	zhè	this		叫	jiào	to be called, call
	那	nà	that		上	shàng	to go to
	什	shén	what		年	nián	year
	么	me	(word ending)		级	jí	grade, level
	吗	ma	(question word)		和	hé	and
	的	de	(possesive particle)		同	tóng	same; together
	不	bù	no, not		学	xué	to study, to learn
6	家	jiā	home	**11**	真	zhēn	really
	有	yǒu	to have, there is/are		饿	è	hungry
	个	gè	(measure word)		吃	chī	to eat
	爸	bà	father		想	xiǎng	to think
	妈	mā	mother		渴	kě	thirsty
	哥	gē	elder brother		喝	hē	to drink
	姐	jiě	elder sister		菜	cài	dish, vegetable
	弟	dì	younger brother		饭	fàn	cooked rice, meal
	妹	mèi	younger sister				

CHINESE EQUIVALENTS OF
ENGLISH NAMES
(a choice from two)

Name	Chinese name				Name	Chinese name			
Aaron	Yèróng	业荣	Yàlún	亚伦	Denise	Díní	笛旎	Dìní	蒂妮
Adam	Yèdēng	业登	Yàdāng	亚当	Denis	Dānní	丹尼	Nísī	尼斯
Adrian	Yějùn	也俊	Yè'ān	业安	Diana	Dài'ān	黛安	Ānnà	安娜
Agnes	Àiní	艾旎	Àinà	爱娜	Donna	Táonà	桃娜	Tángnà	唐娜
Alan	Yělán	野岚	Yàlán	亚蓝	Don	Táng'ēn	唐恩	Duōwén	多闻
Albert	Yèbó	业博	Bótài	伯泰	Dorothy	Táoluò	桃珞	Luòxī	洛曦
Alexander	Yàlì	亚立	Shāndà	山大	Douglas	Dàosī	道思	Lánsī	蓝司
Alexandra	Yǎlì	雅丽	Shānzhuó	姗卓	Duncan	Dūnkěn	敦恳	Dèngkěn	邓肯
Alison, Alice	Yǎlì	雅丽	Lìsī	丽思	Edith	Yísī	怡思	Yīdí	依笛
Amanda	Yǎmàn	雅曼	Měidài	美黛	Edward	Yèdé	业德	Huádé	华德
Amelia	Yǎméi	雅梅	Méilì	玫丽	Elizabeth	Yílì	仪丽	Ruòbèi	若蓓
Amy	Àiméi	爱梅	Àimì	艾蜜	Ellen	Àilíng	蔼玲	Àilín	爱琳
Andrew	Ānzhú	安筑	Ángzhú	昂竹	Emily	Àiméi	爱梅	Měilì	美丽
Andy	Āndí	安笛	Ángdí	昂迪	Emma	Éméi	峨梅	Àimǎ	艾玛
Angela	Yánjí	妍吉	Yànjī	雁姬	Eric	Yíruì	宜瑞	Ruìkè	睿克
Ann	Yànyín	燕吟	Yányīn	妍茵	Ernest	Ēnnǐ	恩拟	Nǐshí	拟实
Annette	Yànní	燕妮	Yánní	妍旎	Frances	Fùlián	馥莲	Xǐsī	喜思
Anthony	Āntóng	安桐	Dōngní	东尼	Francis	Fùlián	富廉	Xīsī	熹斯
April	Àipò	爱珀	Aipú	艾璞	Frank	Fùlián	富廉	Liánkè	廉克
Arnold	Yànuò	亚诺	Ānnài	安耐	Fred	Fúléi	福雷	Lěidé	磊德
Arthur	Yàshū	亚书	Yàsè	亚瑟	Gary	Gēlǐ	歌礼	Jiālǐ	佳理
Barbara	Bābì	芭碧	Bābǐ	巴比	Geoffrey	Jiéfù	杰富	Fúlì	福立
Barry	Bèilǐ	备理	Pèilì	沛立	George	Jiūjí	赳吉	Qiáozhì	乔治
Belinda	Bìlíng	碧玲	Líndá	琳达	Geraldine	Jiéruò	洁若	Ruòtíng	若婷
Ben	Běnēn	本恩	Bèiyí	备宜	Gordon	Gédèng	格邓	Gēdēng	戈登
Benjamin	Bīnjié	斌杰	Jiémǐn	捷敏	Grace	Gēruǐ	歌蕊	Ruìsī	瑞思
Bernard	Běnnà	本纳	Nàdé	纳德	Graham	Gélián	格廉	Ruìmù	睿沐
Beth	Bèishī	贝诗	Bìsī	碧思	Grant	Gélián	革廉	Lántè	岚忒
Betty	Bìdí	碧笛	Bèidì	贝娣	Gregory	Gélěi	格磊	Gélì	格利
Bill	Bìlì	必立	Bǐ'ěr	比尔	Hannah	Hánnài	涵耐	Hánnà	函娜
Bob	Bǎobó	宝柏	Bāobó	包勃	Harold	Hàoruò	浩若	Luòdé	洛德
Bradley	Bǔlěi	卜磊	Léilì	雷利	Harry	Hǎiruì	海瑞	Hàolì	皓立
Brenda	Báilán	白兰	Lándá	兰达	Helen	Hǎilán	海岚	Hǎilún	海伦
Brian	Bǎi'ēn	百恩	Báilán	白岚	Henry	Hànruì	汉瑞	Hēnglì	亨利
Bruce	Bùrú	布儒	Rúshì	儒士	Herbert	Huòbèi	霍碚	Hèbó	贺伯
Bryce	Bǔlài	卜籁	Láishí	莱实	Howard	Héhuá	和华	Hèhuá	贺华
Carol	Kǎiluò	凯珞	Kǎluó	卡罗	Ian	Yí'ān	宜安	Yí'ān	谊安
Caroline	Kǎiluò	凯珞	Luólín	罗琳	Irene	Àilín	爱琳	Àirén	蔼仁
Catharine	Kǎisè	凯瑟	Táolíng	桃玲	Isabel	Yízé	怡则	Bèi'er	蓓儿
Cathy	Kěshī	可诗	Kǎixī	凯西	Ivan	Àiwén	爱文	Àiwén	艾闻
Charles	Chálì	察厉	Chálǐ	查理	Jack	Jiékē	捷珂	Jiékè	杰克
Christine	Kělì	可丽	Sītíng	思婷	Jacqueline	Jiékě	婕可	Kělíng	可玲
Christopher	Kèlì	克历	Tuòfú	拓福	James	Jiànmù	健慕	Jiémǔ	杰姆
Claire	Kěléi	可蕾	Kěruǐ	可蕊	Jane	Jiéyán	婕妍	Jiěyàn	姐雁
Colin	Kèlín	克霖	Kēlín	柯林	Janet	Jiéní	婕旎	Jiéní	洁霓
Connie	Kění	可旎	Kēní	珂旎	Jean	Jíyīn	吉茵	Jīyín	姬吟
Cynthia	Xīnxǐ	欣喜	Xǐyà	喜亚	Jeffery	Jiéfú	捷福	Fùlì	复历
Daniel	Dànní	澹尼	Dānní	丹尼	Jennifer	Zhēnní	珍妮	Nífù	旎馥
David	Dàwěi	大伟	Dàwèi	大卫	Jenny	Zhēnní	真旎	Zhēnní	贞妮
Deborah	Dàibó	黛泊	Bǎolà	宝辣	Jeremy	Jiélè	拮乐	Jiémǐ	杰米

Name	Chinese name				Name	Chinese name			
Jessica	Jiéxī	婕熹	Sījiā	思佳	Patricia	Pèicuì	佩翠	Cuìxiá	翠霞
Jim	Jìmù	纪慕	Jímǔ	吉姆	Patrick	Pèicuī	沛崔	Péicuì	培萃
Joan	Qiūyàn	秋雁	Qiúyán	裘妍	Paul	Bóyí	博宜	Bǎoluó	保罗
Joycelyn	Qiūsī	秋思	Qiūlíng	秋玲	Pauline	Pèilíng	佩玲	Bǎolín	宝琳
John	Jiù'ēn	究恩	Yuēhàn	约翰	Penelope	Pèiluò	佩珞	Luòpí	洛琵
Jonathan	Jiūnà	赳纳	Nánsēn	南森	Peter	Péidé	培德	Bǐdé	彼得
Joseph	Jiūsè	赳瑟	Yàsè	亚瑟	Philip	Fěilì	斐立	Lìpǔ	力圃
Joyce	Qiūyī	秋依	Qiūcí	秋慈	Rachel	Léiqiū	蕾秋	Ruìqiū	瑞秋
Judy	Zhūdì	珠蒂	Zhūdí	茱迪	Raymond	Ruìméng	瑞蒙	Léimèng	雷梦
Judith	Zhūdì	珠蒂	Dísī	笛思	Rebecca	Rúbèi	如蓓	Bèijiā	贝嘉
Julia	Zhūlì	珠丽	Zhūlì	茱莉	Richard	Ruìqí	睿奇	Ruìjiā	瑞佳
Julian	Zhūlián	朱廉	Lǐ'ān	理安	Robert	Ruòbó	若柏	Luóbó	罗勃
June	Zhūyīn	茱茵	Jūnyín	君吟	Robin (f)	Ruòbīng	若冰	Luòbīng	洛冰
Justin	Jiādǐng	佳鼎	Sītǐng	司挺	Robin (m)	Luòbīn	洛斌	Luóbīn	罗彬
Katherine	Kǎilíng	凯玲	Sīlín	思琳	Roger	Luójié	罗杰	Ruòjié	若捷
Kate	Kědí	可笛	Kǎidì	凯娣	Ronald	Lángnuò	琅诺	Lánnà	蓝纳
Kathy	Kěsī	可鸶	Kǎisī	凯思	Rose	Ruòsī	若思	Méiguī	玫瑰
Kay	Kěyí	可怡	Kǎiyí	凯仪	Ross	Luósì	罗似	Luòsī	洛司
Keith	Jìshì	纪适	Jìshí	季实	Roy	Luóyí	罗谊	Luòyī	洛伊
Kenneth	Kēngshí	铿石	Kěnní	恳睨	Russell	Luósù	罗素	Luòsuǒ	洛琐
Larry	Lèruì	乐瑞	Láolí	劳里	Ruth	Rúshì	茹适	Ruòsī	若思
Laura	Lèrú	乐如	Luòruò	珞若	Sally	Shālì	莎莉	Shānlì	姗丽
Lesley	Léisī	蕾思	Léilì	蕾丽	Sam	Sēnmù	森牧	Shānmǔ	山姆
Lilian	Lìlíng	丽玲	Lìlián	丽莲	Sandra	Xiánzhuó	娴倬	Xīndài	欣岱
Lily	Lìli	丽丽	Bǎihé	百合	Sarah	Xiérán	谐然	Xiàrán	夏然
Linda	Líndài	林黛	Líndá	琳达	Scott	Shìkè	世克	Kētè	科忒
Lindsay	Línxī	林曦	Línxī	林熹	Sharon	Xiárán	霞然	Xiàlán	夏兰
Lisa	Lìshā	莉莎	Lìshā	丽沙	Shirley	Xuělì	雪丽	Xuélì	学俐
Lloyd	Luóyì	罗益	Yídé	宜德	Simon	Sàmèng	飒孟	Sàiméng	赛蒙
Louise	Lùyī	露依	Yísī	仪思	Sophia	Sùfěi	素翡	Sūfēi	苏菲
Lucy	Lùxǐ	鹭喜	Lùxī	露西	Stanley	Sītǎn	思坦	Tánlǐ	檀理
Lynn	Línyīn	林茵	Lín	琳	Stephen	Sīdí	思迪	Tìwén	悌文
Margaret	Mǎnruì	满瑞	Mǎgē	玛歌	Stuart	Sīhuá	思华	Sītú	司图
Majorie	Mǎqí	玛祺	Qiūruǐ	秋蕊	Sue	Sùyǐ	素倚	Shūwú	纾梧
Maria	Mǎlì	玛丽	Lìyǎ	丽雅	Susan	Sùrán	素然	Sūshān	苏珊
Mark	Mǎkè	马克	Màikè	迈克	Ted	Tàidé	泰德	Táidí	邰迪
Martin	Màitǐng	迈挺	Mǎdīng	马仃	Teresa	Délì	德莉	Ruìshā	瑞莎
Martha	Mǎshā	玛莎	Měishān	美珊	Terry	Tèlì	特立	Tiělì	铁立
Mary	Méilì	梅丽	Mǎlì	玛丽	Thomas	Tángmù	唐慕	Tángmù	堂睦
Matthew	Méixiū	媚修	Mǎxiū	马修	Tim	Tìmù	悌牧	Dímù	笛慕
Max	Méisì	媚嗣	Màisī	迈思	Tina	Tínà	缇娜	Tíngnà	婷娜
May	Měiyí	美怡	Méiyí	玫宜	Tom	Tuòmù	拓慕	Tāngmǔ	汤姆
Michael	Màikè	迈克	Màikě	麦可	Tony	Tuòní	拓倪	Tōngní	通尼
Michelle	Mìxuě	蜜雪	Xuě'er	雪儿	Tracy	Cuìxǐ	翠喜	Cuìxī	萃西
Nancy	Niànxī	念兮	Nánxī	南西	Veronica	Wéiróng	薇容	Níjiā	旎佳
Natalie	Nǎitáo	芳桃	Táolí	桃莉	Victor	Wěidé	伟德	Wēituò	崴拓
Neville	Níwén	倪文	Wénlǐ	文礼	Victoria	Wěitáo	玮桃	Táolì	桃丽
Nick	Níkè	倪恪	Níkè	尼克	Vicki	Wěiqí	玮琪	Wéiqí	薇绮
Noel	Nuòyōu	诺优	Luó'ěr	罗尔	Vincent	Wénsēn	文森	Wénxīn	闻歆
Norman	Nuòmèng	诺孟	Luòméng	珞蒙	Virginia	Wěiqín	玮琴	Qínyǎ	琴雅
Oliver	Àolì	傲立	Àolǐ	奥理	Vivian	Wěiwén	玮文	Wéiwén	薇雯
Owen	Wòwén	斡闻	Ōuwén	欧文	Wendy	Yuándí	嫒笛	Wéndì	文娣
Pamela	Péiméi	培玫	Báiméi	白梅	William	Wěilín	伟林	Wēilián	威廉
Pam	Pèiméi	佩梅	Péiměi	培美	Yvonne	Yīfán	依帆	Yìfāng	怡芳